W9-BAV-979

CANDLESTICKS

Title page illustration
Engraving by and after Frans Bleyswyck. An illustration to one of the poems of Jacob Zeuss
(*Gedichten van Jakob Zeuss,* two volumes, Delft, 1721).

CANDLESTICKS

Geoffrey Wills

Clarkson N. Potter, Inc./Publisher   NEW YORK

DISTRIBUTED BY CROWN PUBLISHERS, INC

Library of Congress Catalog Card Number: 73-88646
ISBN: 0-517-514141
First American edition published in 1974 by Clarkson N. Potter, Inc.
Printed in Great Britain

Contents

Foreword

Candlesticks, like poems, are plentiful and beautiful, and compiling a book about them has proved tantamount to making an anthology of verse. In both cases it is as difficult to decide what to include as what to omit, and the result is a personal selection.

In the present instance I have covered many periods and countries, showing the various materials used and the styles in which they were made. Apart from a few of the very earliest examples it will be seen that all have artistic merit to a great or lesser degree. In conformity with that I have excluded the rustic iron candlestick, which was seldom more than purely functional and remained largely unchanged over the centuries.

The book is divided into two separate sections: one dealing with the subject of the title, candlesticks, and the other with their *raison d'être*, candles. Both are bound up with social and economic history, and their stories are interwoven.

G. W.

Acknowledgements

The illustrations have been gathered from numerous sources, public and private, and the author acknowledges the kindness of the undermentioned owners and guardians in allowing the photographs to be reproduced:

Messrs Ader, Picard and Tajan, Paris

Kurt Albrecht (Kozminsky Galleries Pty Ltd), Melbourne

American Museum in Britain, Claverton Manor, Bath

Bearnes and Waycotts, Torquay, Devon

Christie's, London

City Museum and Art Gallery, Plymouth

Delomosne and Son Ltd, London

Mrs Una des Fontaines

King and Chasemore, Pulborough, Sussex

Manchester City Art Gallery: Thomas Greg Collection

Mansell Collection, London

Metropolitan Museum of Art, New York: gift of Ann Payne Blumenthal, 1939; gift of Robert L. Cammann, 1957; bequest of A. T. Clearwater, 1933; Cloisters Collection, 1947; gift of Mrs Emily Winthrop Miles, 1946; gift of Anna G. W. Green, in memory of Dr Charles W. Green

Earl of Mount Edgcumbe

The National Trust: Saltram, Devon

Parke-Bernet Galleries, Inc, New York

Phillips, London

Sheffield City Museum

Sotheby's, London

Spink and Son Ltd, London

Trustees of the Wallace Collection, London

Josiah Wedgwood and Sons Ltd, Etruria, Staffordshire

Victoria & Albert Museum, London

Candlesticks through the centuries

The function of the candlestick has always been, basically, simply to hold a candle in a position of safety, so as to avoid damage by fire from the flame and prevent mess from molten wax or grease – the dangers inseparable from a naked light of this kind. Indeed, a prudent eighteenth-century lady, Mrs Whatman, noted that 'the first thing a housekeeper should teach her new servant is to carry her candle upright'. Over the years, the candlestick has taken innumerable forms, ranging from the crude pad of clay with which a miner stuck a taper to his headgear or a nearby wall, to the elaborately-designed gold and silver objects created for more sophisticated surroundings. In between these extremes there have been many hundreds of thousands of candlesticks made from a wide range of materials. Some of them have been preserved complete, or damaged, while of others no traces remain except a painting, drawing or engraving or a few words of description.

Over the centuries, candlesticks have been confused with candelabra, wall-lights and chandeliers; in addition, a distinction has not always been clearly drawn between a holder for an oil-lamp and one for a candle. A case in point is that biblical seven-branched candelabrum, or menorah, provided by Moses for the Ark of the Covenant. It was described in the Book of Exodus (chapter 37, verse 17) as a 'candlestick of pure gold' ornamented with flowers and knops, the latter being rounded studs or bosses. It was further stated to have had 'six branches going out of the sides thereof; three branches of the candlestick out of the one side thereof, and three branches of the candlestick out of the other side thereof'. It had, in fact, one central support and two sets of three side branches, each of the seven holding a small vessel containing oil and a wick.

The first candlesticks would have been the most simple of functional objects in which to place a burning candle to hold it upright: no more than a piece of wood or stone with a hollow cut into it, or fitted with a spike of some kind to form a pricket. Such plain items possessed no artistic merit, so there was no feature about them, other than that of utility, to ensure their preservation for more than a limited time. If damaged they would be cast aside without compunction, and quickly replaced by something of similar type.

Apart from those used by the Romans, the earliest candlesticks of general interest date from the eleventh and twelfth centuries. Like the majority of those made during the ensuing two or three hundred years they were for ecclesiastical use. For that reason, especial care was taken over their design and manufacture, and in most instances they represented the best craftmanship of their day.

A pair of silver candlesticks is recorded as having been presented to Westminster Abbey in about the year 1250 by Henry III, while some two centuries later Henry VI owned a pair made 'of gold set with four sapphires, four rubies, four emeralds and twenty-four pearls'. It was not until after the Restoration in 1660, with the accession to the throne of Charles II, that silver candlesticks were made in any quantity, and surviving specimens of earlier date from England or any other country are scarce.

Wars and other disorders have periodically resulted in the destruction of valuables, not least those belonging to the church. Gold and silver, which are easily melted to become unrecognisable and negotiable, have always been prime targets for the unscrupulous. A further cause of heavy loss has been successive changes in fashion, which resulted in the re-making of older, outmoded articles into those considered to be more useful and acceptable to the then-prevailing taste. There was not always the present-day reverence for anything old, meritorious or not, and an heir did not hesitate to dispose of inherited possessions in return for others of more modern pattern.

MANUFACTURE

Surviving eleventh- and twelfth-century examples are made of brass or bronze. These metals, alloys of copper with zinc and with tin, respectively, have been known to mankind for many thousands of years. Their manufacture in the past centred on places offering good supplies of the essential constituents as well as of the fuel essential to melt them. The various areas also attracted craftsmen able to form the metal into finished goods, and these men passed on their skills from generation to generation.

Copper and brass were actively traded from country to country, with the miners of Germany acquiring an international reputation for their knowledge and proficiency. In England, some of the ample deposits of copper were worked by the Romans, but it was the importation of German workers under Elizabeth I that eventually led to full exploitation of the neglected source of wealth. Up to the late seventeenth century production remained limited for one reason and another, and much of the copper required for domestic use, as well as most of the brass, was imported from across the English Channel. This material was often referred to as 'battery metal' because it was supplied in plates beaten to the required thinness by means of mechanical hammers worked by water-power. Alternatively it was known as 'latten'.

From time to time both miners and metal-workers crossed the borders dividing countries, and duly settled where conditions were more attractive. They brought technical skill in addition to a knowledge of the varieties and patterns of goods popular in their native lands. Thus it is not always possible to be certain of the exact origin of many pieces; a circumstance common to almost all the applied arts.

In the manufacture of candlesticks and other articles little use was made of the metals in a pure state: gold, silver and copper all require alloying to render them durable. Brass, bronze and gun-metal, the last being a mixture of copper and tin but in different proportions from those of bronze, were commonly employed. In some instances gold and silver and the copper alloys were hammered into shape from flat sheets, but just as often they were cast from the solid metal, the molten material being poured into shaped moulds. Frequent use was made of the 'lost wax' (*cire perdue*) process, from which the ancient Greeks and Romans had obtained notable results: a slightly undersized rough model of the desired object is made of clay and over it is poured wax, which is carefully hand-finished in full detail. A clay covering is applied, and the whole heated so that the wax can be poured out and replaced by

Dutch brass-workers. An engraving from a book published in Amsterdam in 1718.

molten metal. After the whole has cooled, the outer casing is broken away and the inner clay core picked out. A drawback to the process is that only a single cast is obtainable from the wax original, and to make duplicates the entire operation must be repeated.

Shapes could also be formed by pouring the metal into suitable simple moulds of sand and clay. These were limited in application to objects of straightforward shape like bells, bowls and so forth, having no undercut ornament to prevent their removal from the mould. *Cire perdue* was reserved for articles of complex design which could be given thin walls, and so ensure an economical use of the metal concerned. In all instances further hand-work was necessary for the clarification of detail blurred or clogged in the making, the degree of finish varying according to the skill of the craftsman and the destination of the piece.

Objects made from sheet metal could also be decorated by carefully hammering a pattern into the surface or from the underside. Such embossing, chasing or repoussé work was usually a combination of several techniques including engraving.

Colour could be added by means of enamel, composed of coloured glass ground to a powder and treated to give it a lower melting-point than normal. The object to be decorated was cast with a series of hollows, or else these could be cut out later (champlevé), or they were formed by soldering on the surface a series of wire walls (cloisonné). In both cases, champlevé and cloisonné, the hollow places were filled with the powder, which melted at about 800°C and flowed to fill the spaces. Finally the enamel was ground down to the level of the encircling narrow walls of metal. The processes were known in early times and revived in the Middle Ages, when they were practised in France and Germany with success. The craftsmen of Limoges, in west-central France, became particularly adept at exploiting champlevé, while cloisonné was a speciality of the Chinese and Japanese. At Limoges, from the late fifteenth century onwards, a fresh process came into use: a very thin sheet of copper or other pure metal was beaten to the desired shape, covered all over with a coating of enamel and after firing was further embellished with painting in the same medium, but in contrasting colours. With judicious control of temperature and repetitions of the procedure for individual colours, it was possible to prevent the tints from intermingling. Each colour melted at a different heat and as neither the thermometer nor the pyrometer had yet been invented, the result depended on the judgement of the maker. The work of the best exponents of the art has the appearance of a fine quality miniature-painting, betraying no sign of the great skill and experience involved in its making.

Much use was made of surface gilding, not only to prevent tarnish and save the labour of periodical polishing, but to give an object an impressive and beautiful appearance. It was known and used from an early period in many countries, and was applicable to silver as well as to copper and its alloys. Briefly, gilding was performed by mixing granulated gold with mercury to form an amalgam that was then applied to the cleaned surface of the article. Heating drove off the mercury in the form of a poisonous vapour and left the gold evenly distributed. It could remain matt or be burnished, in part or wholly, or could be left contrastingly part-dull, part-shiny. Alternatively, the gold might appear only on selected portions of an article; it was then described as part- or 'parcel-gilt'. In the eighteenth century French workers became extremely skilled at the work, and their gilt-bronze (ormolu) was pre-eminent. It was rivalled closely by the productions of Matthew Boulton, of Birmingham.

Silver could also be imitated in appearance. Polished pewter, a mixture of tin with other metals, resembled it but lacked its durability, whereas the imported alloy, Paktong, has been described as 'very hard and tough and is not easily corroded'. It was made from a mixture of copper, nickel and zinc, and was brought from China during the eighteenth century to be made into fire-grates, fenders, candlesticks and other objects. It was sometimes referred to as Tutenag, and under either name was expensive.

With the invention in the 1740s of Sheffield plate, it became possible to make articles of comparatively inexpensive copper and give them a fused surface of silver, so it might be thought they were silver throughout. In time it was found that the thin upper surface wore away to reveal the pink colour of the metal beneath, and a number of silvery-coloured substitutes for the copper were introduced. Under various names, such as Britannia metal, German silver and nickel silver, they were produced in immense quantities. After 1840 the silver was deposited electrically, and in due course articles were stamped with the initials E.P.N.S. to denote that they were made of electro-plated nickel silver. However, such marking often bore a superficial likeness to that on silver, which was a guarantee of the standard of purity of the precious metal. Despite the protests of silversmiths, makers of plate were not halted in their dubious practice.

Candlesticks that have withstood the hazards of several intervening centuries had their origins in many countries. The earliest of them, as might be expected, bear only slight although often interesting artistic embellishment. A notable exception is the Gloucester candlestick (Plate 1); its date of manufacture is well authenticated, though its precise origin has been debated. At present the controversy has largely died down and the piece is widely assumed to have been made in England. In striking contrast to most other objects surviving from so long ago, in this case the twelfth century, much of the history of the candlestick is known. Not surprisingly there are gaps during which it was completely lost sight of, but the recorded facts undoubtedly add greatly to its interest both historically and artistically.

The decoration of the Gloucester candlestick, with its elaborate pattern of realistic men, monsters and foliage, is comparable to illustrations in manuscripts executed at about the same date. Some of these were produced in England, but similar work was being done elsewhere. It is a commonplace today that fashions of all kinds are quickly copied in one country after another, and this is usually ascribed to the use of photography, the telephone and modern forms of transport. Even without these aids the same seems to have occurred centuries ago, so that what was currently the mode in one centre was almost immediately imitated and adapted hundreds of miles away.

The Gloucester candlestick is unique, but others of quite different pattern survive from about the same date. They were made in northern Europe, especially in the area of Dinant, on the river Meuse, an important source of fine metalwork. The terms 'Dinanderie' and 'Mosan', derived from the town and the river respectively, are sometimes applied to antique brass and bronze articles which originated there.

The production of silver candlesticks was as widespread as that of examples in cheaper metals, although it was more limited in quantity on account of the expense involved. While supplies of silver came at first from European mines, they were later augmented by immense amounts imported into Spain from America. The galleons laden with bullion returning to their home ports were tempting targets for English and other adventurers, who were active in diverting their cargoes to the treasuries of Queen Elizabeth and her fellow monarchs. William Harrison, whose *Description of England* was published in 1577 and revised 10 years later, noted a big increase in prosperity compared with a few decades earlier. He wrote:

> Certes in noblemen's houses it is not rare to see . . . rich hangings of tapestry, silver vessel, and so much other plate as may furnish sundry cupboards to the sum oftentimes of a thousand or two thousand pounds at the least, whereby the value of this and the rest of their stuff doth grow to be almost inestimable.

The same applied, according to Harrison, to other wealthy citizens of the time, as well as to 'inferior artificers and many farmers' who have, for the most part, learned also to garnish their cupboards with plate . . . whereby the wealth of our country (God be praised therefore, and give us grace to employ it well) doth infinitely appear'.

The majority of silverware dating from Tudor times or earlier has disappeared, but the painstakingly-compiled inventories of plate and jewellery belonging to Elizabeth I are an important source of information on it. The lists were compiled between 1570 and 1594, and include not only the hereditary possessions of the Tudor Queen, but gifts received by her during these years.

Of the 1605 items in the published volume, only three have so far been identified as surviving: the latest a silver-gilt table-salt of French make which was brought to light in 1967.

Among the numerous long-lost objects are a number of candlesticks, of which the most remarkable was a set of three given to Henry VIII by Catherine of Aragon. A fourth was added to them at a later date, and in 1570 they were listed as follows:

> Foure Candelstickes of golde with prickes [prickets: spikes] for a Table garnisshed with H and R enamelid red well wrought.

These were unique, but while others then in Royal ownership may have been less valuable historically and intrinsically they are nonetheless interesting. Included among them was a set of six of silver-gilt fitted with sockets, and for which there were the same number of prickets so that they were usable in either form. There were also a number described in only a few words apiece, sufficient to show the variety of their ornament. Typical were:

> Two faire Candlestickes guilt with square sockettes ther bodies with Scalloppes

And:

> Two Candelstickes of Christall garnisshid with siluer and guilt

The last pair may have resembled the pair in Plate 21, which bear the Paris silver marks for 1583-4. The origin of the Royal pair cannot be determined, but it could well have been France. The interchangeability of the terms 'candlestick' and 'chandelier' is shown by a further series of entries: six 'Chaundellors' of 1570 had been noted earlier as 'Candlestickes', and when two of them were later lost they were recorded as 'Chaundlers'. All the afore-mentioned articles were apparently mislaid or deliberately consigned to the melting-pot long ago. Even if most of the Royal treasures had not been sent to the Mint to be converted into coin, as was the case, daily wear and tear over a period of four centuries would equally have ensured their disappearance. But there is always the hope that some recorded item may yet be identified after being overlooked for centuries.

The seventeenth century saw the virtual eclipse of the pricket for domestic use, and from then onwards it was confined to places of worship. At the same time candlesticks were made with wide spreading bases that guaranteed stability, and centrally-placed pans to catch drips of wax or fat. Accidental fire was an ever-present danger, and as the use of candles became more general they must have been the cause of an increasing number of conflagrations. Thus, candle-holders were heavily constructed to prevent them being knocked over unintentionally, and this lends them an imposing appearance. Their sturdy design has no doubt led to the preservation of a fair number of examples that might otherwise have been thrown aside.

In the British Isles there has been no repetition of the wholesale melting of silverware of all kinds that took place during the Civil War of the 1640s, although on two occasions in the present century the energetic and patriotic collection of less precious metals for conversion into munitions took its toll of candlesticks among much else. In France a comparable despoiling of fine silver articles occurred during the Revolution in the late eighteenth century, and in that country as well as in others on the European mainland there have been continual wars. On these occasions, especially between 1939 and 1945, much that was not surrendered to the Ministry was destroyed by military action.

By the early eighteenth century most candlesticks were shaped and ornamented so that they might take their place among the other decorative
objects in a home, and ecclesiastical influence on their design came to an end.
The first examples of the period set a style by shedding the prominent broad
central grease-pan and replacing it with a narrow pan at the top of the stem,

A rich candlestick or girandole, 'which
if executed in Wood gilt, in burnish'd
Gold, or Brass, would be extremely
grand, and might be equally the same
executed in Silver, proper for a Stand or
Marble Table'. From *The Universal
System of Household Furniture,* by William Ince and John Mayhew, London
cabinet-makers, published *c.* 1762.

while the trumpet-shaped base became flattened in form and made round or octagonal to suit the buyer. Ornamentation was often confined to an engraved crest or coat of arms, but in France the motifs of the current Baroque style were employed. These were cast and engraved on examples in silver-gilt and gilt-bronze, taking the form of stiffly-drawn panels of diaper within borders of strapwork with an occasional use of leaves, shells and medallions (Plate 43).

One of the features of the work of some of the Baroque artists and designers was a less formal employment of a number of its elements. A few of them introduced figures of monkeys in the roles of humans (*singeries*), which resulted in a gayer effect than was usual. This was developed, together with a modification of the classically severe overall appearance, and a fresh style, the rococo, came into being.

The word rococo derives from the French *rocaille*: rocks, in allusion to the extensive employment in the style of natural forms such as rocks, plants, water and so forth. The various details were united by curves, their ends curled so that they resembled the letter 'C', and the whole effect is one of movement, compared with the rigidity of the preceding fashion. In addition, the sense of mobility was accentuated by a studied asymmetry: a complete disregard of balance, so that the two sides of a mirror-frame, for instance, were no longer required to match each other (Plate 47).

These features of the rococo were adapted to suit the tastes of different countries. In Germany and Italy they were often carried to extremes, while others, including England, often modified them to a locally-acceptable level of eccentricity. Among the exceptions to this, many of the designs of the London carver Thomas Johnson rival in their extravagance much that was produced elsewhere in Europe. Even the staid firm of Ince & Mayhew, designers and cabinet-makers, whose book of designs issued in about 1762 showed what was then modish, went so far as to include the candlestick on page 17.

By 1760 the rococo had been in vogue for the best part of 20 years, and the first signs of a change were becoming apparent. Just as the pendulum of fashion had earlier swung violently away from classicism, this time it swung back to it in a similar manner. The new version became known, appropriately, as the 'neo-classic', linked inseparably with the name and career of the Scottish-born architect, Robert Adam.

It has for long been debated whether neo-classicism originated in France or England. The sources of its neat swags of flowers, husks and leaves, paterae (round or oval ornamented discs), winged griffins and other motifs were ancient Greece and Rome. The motifs were now re-employed in a precise manner, in complete contrast to the disorder of rococo. Knowledge of the classical past had been accumulating during most of the eighteenth century, having received a notable stimulus when the ruins of the city of Herculaneum, near Naples, began to be excavated. Then in 1748 came the location of the site of Pompeii, overwhelmed with nearby Herculaneum when Vesuvius erupted in AD 79, and the gradual publication of what was found there. By the early 1760s a few French designers had begun to anticipate public interest in the earlier civilisation, and some Paris notables were having their homes decorated in the new style. Very shortly afterwards it spread to England.

Neo-classicism, of course, affected the design of candlesticks, many being given the silhouette of elongated Greek vases or being formed as miniature columns, usually Corinthian, often more slender and somewhat taller than their predecessors. In England, there was ornamentation in the form of engraved husks and other motifs, but in France and Italy less restraint was shown. The Louis XVI style, which was more or less common to both countries, often approached the elaboration of the rococo, but with straight lines or gentle curves replacing the abandon and asymmetry.

As the century progressed, the arts of Greece and Rome continued to influence the West, and a deeper study of the culture of the Mediterranean area resulted in a more academic approach to the ornament once employed there. It increased the number of motifs available, while many of the newer furnishings were almost perfect copies of those used by the ancients. In addition, the spectacular careers of Napoleon, Wellington, Nelson and others, whose military and naval exploits were the centre of the western world's attention affected the non-martial arts. The French emperor's predilection for visualising himself as a follower of the Caesars gave the French 'Empire' style a strong flavour of Imperial Rome. His venture into Egypt in 1798, together with Nelson's victory of the Nile of the same year, introduced a taste in both France and England for sphinxes, crocodiles and obelisks. The range was further widened north of the Channel by the Prince Regent's admiration for Oriental art, testified by the Pavilion at Brighton and by much of its specially-designed contents. Thus, the near-parallel French Empire and English Regency periods saw candlesticks made in a great variety of patterns and, it may be added, by craftsmen whose skill was unequalled.

Just as the early nineteenth-century styles were more complex than those they succeeded, so the later ones of about 1820-40 were even more elaborate. The purity of classicism that had once been the goal of designers was supplanted by revivals of rococo and by motifs taken from other once-popular styles: in France that of François I and in England that of the Tudors and also one more of the sporadic outbursts of Gothic (Plate 90). As the harnessing of steam-power developed and machines were devised to perform operations that had formerly been executed by hand much artistic endeavour was stifled. Mass-production began to replace craftsman-made goods, and the demands of the multitude assumed a greater importance than the more cultivated tastes of the few.

As the candle was rapidly replaced by gas and oil, the candlestick gradually lost its former importance and the attention paid to its design diminished. In the last quarter of the nineteenth century there arose a revival of interest in plain furnishings and rustic simplicity initiated by William Morris and his co-workers, but those subscribing to it saw no reason to put the hands of the clock back in every way. A return to candlelight, however romantic it may have been thought, was of limited attraction in the face of modern illuminants. Thenceforward the candle was reserved for the poor, for use in religious ceremonies, as a reliable standby in emergencies, and to provide a relaxing atmosphere at the dinner-table.

POTTERY, PORCELAIN AND GLASS

The greatest number of surviving candlesticks are made of metal, either precious or base. Artistically, those of the former are the most interesting; the intrinsic value of the materials demanding the employment of more skilful designers and craftsmen. As an alternative to metal, glass and pottery were used from the mid-seventeenth century, and within a hundred years porcelain added a further choice.

The potters, a term embracing also the makers of porcelain, imitated the shapes of silver and brass, and were additionally able to colour their wares attractively and without difficulty. When these newer materials were introduced their cost often rivalled that of silver. Nonetheless they were in keen demand: not only the price but the fragility of glass, pottery and porcelain was overlooked. Their scarcity today is no indication of the very large quantities of candlesticks made from all three materials and subsequently discarded.

The French were foremost in Europe in their admiration for porcelain and in efforts to enhance and preserve it. They did this by mounting examples from all countries in gilt-bronze (ormolu), so that the metalwork provided a frame for the object and also protected it from damage. The fashion for such work spread to Germany, and sometimes the mounts made there are indistinguishable from the French. Much of the German ormolu, however, is of comparatively poor quality, with weak designs carried out in metal with thin gilding. In England there was a more worthy attempt to rival Paris in the art, with Matthew Boulton, of the Soho Manufactory, Birmingham, devoting some of his energies to the task. His identified work, of which more is being found as a result of research, is of excellent quality.

Boulton's friend, Josiah Wedgwood, the potter, was requested to sell him wares suitable for mounting, but was diffident in complying. Some pairs of candlesticks and cassolettes (small vases with lids reversing to form candle-holders) are attributed to Boulton. Many of them are made in part of Derbyshire fluorspar; known also as 'Blue John', the stone shows a distinctive purple in combination with other colours, and is set off to advantage by the gilt metal.

Wedgwood made an interesting comment on the fashion for mounting in a letter he wrote in 1763 to his partner, Thomas Bentley. The former was in London at the time, and he recorded:

> Mr Boulton tells me I should be surprised to know what a trade has lately been made out of vases in Paris. The artists have even come over to London, picked up all the old whimsical ugly things they could meet with, carried them to Paris, where they have mounted and ornamented them with metal. . . .

Wedgwood jasperware drum for mounting as the base of a candlestick, as in plate 78. (*Josiah Wedgwood & Sons, Ltd.*)

Dick Swiveller, in Charles Dickens's *The Old Curiosity Shop*, in bed playing the flute by the light of a candle, the latter in a chamber candlestick supported on an upturned top-hat. A woodcut after a drawing by Hablot Knight Browne, known as 'Phiz', published in 1840.

Most common in France and Germany, only occasionally carried out in England, was the setting of a porcelain figure on a gilt-metal base from which rose a support terminating in a candle-holder. As early as the 1750s the Bow porcelain factory, situated on the fringe of London, gave many of their figures and groups a square hole at the back to simplify the task of the metal-worker. Later, English and a few other potters raised their figures on scrolled bases and gave them candle-arms of porcelain; emulating those of metal so that ormolu was not required for the purpose (Plates 66 and 67).

There were a number of deviations from the basic candlestick, the most familiar being the chamber-stick, which was carried about. In its usual form it has a deep and wide tray with a central short stem beneath the candle-holder. The tray is fitted with a vertical ring handle or a flat one like that of a saucepan, and there is often a conical extinguisher with a slot to hold it when not in use. In country districts such articles were regularly employed until well into the first half of the present century, but the spread of electricity meant their end. Chamber candlesticks were made of many of the materials already mentioned, and large numbers were turned out cheaply in tinned, painted and enamelled sheet iron.

Shades were sometimes provided for candles, especially when they were to be used in entrance halls or elsewhere where draughts were likely. In that case, so-called wind- or hurricane-covers of glass would be employed (Plate 99), but being obviously fragile they are now scarce. Some of the French ormolu candlesticks were made so that the candle-holder was backed by a tall upright rod on which would slide a flat silk-covered shade. It adjusted up or down, according to the length of the candle and height of its flame, so that a user's eyes were shielded from glare. An English version of a comparable device was described and illustrated in the *Gentleman's Magazine* in 1746 (see on right).

Perhaps something of a similar kind was referred to earlier, in 1743, by Mrs Elizabeth Purefoy. Writing from her home near Buckingham to a London cabinet-maker she told him:

> A gentleman & gentlewoman who came to our house liked your candle stick (with a Tin thing to hide the candle) so well that they would have each of them one. So I desire you will send two of those candlesticks. . . .

Samuel Pepys, who was always keenly interested in whatever was new to him, was much impressed by the words of an engraver, Edward Cocker, who told him that the best light for his fine work was provided by a candle 'set to advantage, as he could do it'. In October 1664 the diarist noted:

> Came Mr Cocker, and brought me a globe of glass and a frame of oiled paper, as I desired, to show me the manner of his gaining light to grave by, and to lessen the glaringness of it at pleasure by an oiled paper. This I bought of him, giving him a crown for it; and so well satisfied, he went away.

The glass globe was filled with water so that it acted as a condensing lens and concentrated the candle-light on a small area. Lamps like this were used also by lacemakers, jewellers and others requiring a vivid spot of illumination rather than an overall even level of brightness.

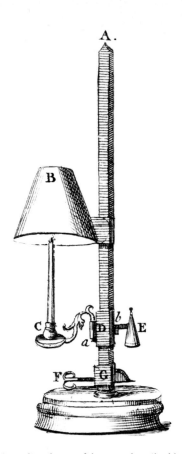

A reading-lamp of the type described by Mrs Purefoy as a 'candlestick (with a Tin thing to hide the candle)'. From an engraving published in 1746.

EJECTORS AND ADJUSTERS

The difficulty of removing the stub of a used candle received attention from many inventive minds. Not only could a fresh candle not be inserted in the holder until the old one had been taken away, but the economical could re-melt the recovered piece. At first it was sufficient to have a hole, circular or shaped, at the side of the socket so that a short length of wire or stick could be inserted to prize up the stub (Plate 25). This was common during much of the seventeenth century and was thought to have originated in the Netherlands; indeed all candlesticks with this feature were at one time called Flemish or Dutch. It is now considered impossible to state where anything so simple might have been first thought of and used, and it is no longer regarded as a reliable basis for attribution.

In the early years of the eighteenth century the hollow stems of many brass and bronze candlesticks were fitted with ejectors worked by pushing upwards a button placed centrally under the base (opposite). The button was fixed to a rod running up the inside of the stem, which terminated in a flat disc resting in the base of the candle-socket: a simple device that is easier to use than to describe. A variation of it had a short lever projecting through a slot in the side of the stem, obviating the necessity of turning the candlestick upside-down to use the ejector.

The last variety of ejector was to be found in inexpensive tinned-iron candlesticks popular during the nineteenth century, when they were greatly favoured on farmsteads in the United States; they earned the nickname 'hog-scrapers', because it was said that their owners found the sharp rim of the base a good substitute for a razor in removing bristles from hog hides.

From at least the eighteenth century, thought was devoted to maintaining the light-source at a constant level, a convenience far more efficiently achieved by the oil-lamp. With the lace-maker's condenser, either the globe or the candle had to be adjusted constantly to keep the light where it was required. Various elementary candlesticks were given sockets that adjusted up or down, being retained in position by a lever in the stem pressing against a notch. A more satisfactory solution to the problem was to enclose the candle in a metal tube with a hole at the top through which the wick protruded. In the base of the tube was a steel spring keeping the candle pressed upwards, and in consequence the flame was always in the same position instead of falling as the candle was consumed.

The device was revived in the nineteeth century, when it was found that the metal round the top, holding the candle in place, kept the curling wick from contact with the candle's edge. Guttering was thereby eliminated, and it was possible to burn tallow candles, which normally required constant snuffing.

The ejector button under the base of an 18th-century brass candlestick. The button is fitted to a rod running up inside the stem, and has a flat disc at the upper end which pushes out the candle stub.

23

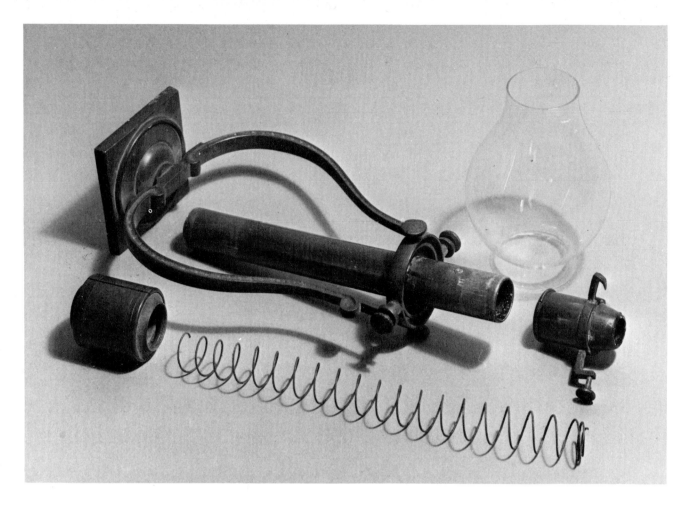

The prices of candlesticks of any particular material or type varied over the years according to the cost of materials, labour, transport and other factors. Silver ones, for instance, could cost little or much according to the design and the amount of metal involved, so that no satisfactory guide can be given. Candlesticks of brass and similar metals are no less difficult to list, as records of their cost are few and far between. Two may be quoted, one in the United States and the other in England. The first appeared in *Rivington's New-York Gazeteer* of 28 September 1775:

> Fifes and Sword knots to be had at the Printers's:
> Also Handsome Brass Candlesticks at 22s., 18s. 6d. and 16s. a pair.

Probably these had been imported, because it was not for some years after the close of the War of Independence that citizens of the (newly-formed) United States began to establish enough of their own manufactories to cease to rely on goods brought from Europe. The other quotation is from the autobiography of Joseph Brasbridge, a retail silversmith with premises in Fleet Street, London, at the end of the eighteenth century. His prosy account reveals that the arts of buying and selling remain unaltered during some 200 years:

> A gentleman came into my shop, as he was passing by, for a pair of plated candlesticks: he fixed on a pair, the price of which was four and thirty shillings [£1·70: about $4.20]. He said that he did not intend to lay out more than a guinea and a half [£1·57½: about $3.75], and asked me if I

A 19th-century bronze candlestick showing its component parts, including the steel spring to keep the candle flame at a constant height while it burns. The candlestick is seen assembled in plate 112.

would let him have them for that sum. I told him it was contrary to my plan to make any abatement. He replied, that he did not come to me for plans, but for candlesticks; I then told him that I would give up my plan for his; but that I hoped the next time he came into my shop the word abatement would not be mentioned. He replied that his *plan* at that moment was to give the candlesticks to Captain Fraser, the commissary at Dunkirk, appointed by government to superintend the demolition of the fortifications there, at the end of that war. He added, that he had another *plan* in his head, which he would tell me the next time he came. Accordingly he procured me orders from Captain Fraser, at different times, for between three and four hundred pairs of candlesticks similar to those which I first sent to him. . . .

As to how much should be paid for the same candlesticks today, it is almost impossible to say. The prices fluctuate over the years along with other antiques. The purchaser of candlesticks must be guided by his taste and his pocket; two factors that unfortunately do not always go together. One point may be emphasised: candlesticks should preferably be acquired in sets, usually the twos or fours in which they were originally sold. Not only are they then more effective for display, but they are then more valuable. Single examples command under half the cost of a pair, and while there is always a long chance that one will at some time be matched with its twin, this is little more probable than pairing off an odd cup with a saucer of the same pattern.

There can be little doubt that the candle and its holder will be with us into the forseeable future. In the twentieth century we are accustomed to the convenience of light at the touch of a switch, but as with all things there is a constant possibility of failure for some reason, mechanical or human – and a persistent appreciation of the relaxing allure of candlelight at the dinner-table. Thus, the candlestick will retain, as it has for so many hundreds of years, a place in the home in both a decorative and a practical capacity.

Illustrations

1 The Gloucester Candlestick. This early 12th-century candlestick, made of gilt bell-metal, is claimed to be of English manufacture not only because of its unique design but on account of its history. The wording on the stem states that it was presented to the church (now the cathedral) of Gloucester, in about the year AD 1100. An ancient inscription on it records that it was later given to the French cathedral of Le Mans, from where it disappeared during the French Revolution. In 1861 it was offered for sale by a collector and was bought for the Victoria & Albert Museum, where it may be seen and admired. Height 58.4 cm. *Victoria & Albert Museum*.

2 A bronze candlestick made in the 12th century in Khorassan, a province of the old Persian Empire, now Iran. The hexagons round the deep base are embossed with sphinxes, hares and palm-leaves; while round the borders are lions, seated at the top and running at the lower edge. Diameter 38 cm. *Christie's.*

3 A brass pricket candlestick modelled in the shape of a bird supporting on its back the candle-holder, which is reinforced by a scroll-pattern at the base. It was probably made in Lorraine in the 12th century. Height 24.5 cm. *Victoria & Albert Museum.*

4 A late 12th-century bronze candle-stick, thought to have been made in Lorraine, a province in the region of the river Meuse. The imaginative figure combines the body of a bird with the tail of a fish, the legs of a lion and the upper portion of a man, who is depicted holding a scrolled branch forming a handle. The pricket has been restored. Height 19 cm. *Victoria & Albert Museum.*

5 A pair of 13th-century French pricket candlesticks of gilt copper, the patterns in champlevé enamel. The three feet supporting each of them are decorated with ogres' heads. *Metropolitan Museum of Art, New York: The Cloisters Collection, purchased 1947.*

1 Pair of silver candlesticks, London, about 1700. Numerous makers were responsible for others of similar pattern between about 1685 and 1710. Height 17.1 cm. *Private collection.*

2 Pair of enamel candlesticks with pierced drip-pans, made at a South Staffordshire factory in about 1765. Height 24.7 cm. *City Museum and Art Gallery, Plymouth.*

3 Plymouth porcelain groups of two children posed against a flowering shrub or 'bocage' background. The factory was established at Plymouth, England, in 1768, but after only a couple of years was removed to Bristol so examples are scarce. Height 21.2 cm. *City Museum and Art Gallery, Plymouth.*

4 Pewter candlestick bearing the mark of Bush and Perkins, who were working in Bristol in about 1775. The design is unusual and at a glance might be thought to be a century older than it is. Height 17.1 cm.
Private collection.

5 Pair of candlesticks with cut-glass bodies and hanging drops, dating from the Regency period, about 1820. Height 16.5 cm. *Private collection*.

6 Pair of Sheffield plate, silver on copper, candlesticks with telescopic stems. They date from about 1830. Height 20.8 cm. *City Museum and Art Gallery, Plymouth.*

7 Stoneware candlestick with incised and coloured ornament, made by R. W. Martin and his brothers in about 1880. Their pottery was at Southall and they had a London showroom in Brownlow Street, Holborn. Height 17.7 cm. *City Museum and Art Gallery, Plymouth.*

8 Chamber candlestick of Staffordshire pottery with blue-printed decoration of an Oriental scene. Made in about 1830 by one of the numerous factories competing to supply ware of this type. Overall width 14 cm. *City Museum and Art Gallery, Plymouth.*

9 Machine-made pressed glass chamber candlestick, embossed appropriately with the words '*Good Night*'. It was probably made in the Newcastle-upon-Tyne area about 1890. Width 10.5 cm. *Private collection.*

6 A bronze pricket candlestick with a curved triangular base, spirally-twisted stem with a central knop, and a drip-pan resembling a coronet. The feet have been grievously maltreated: they should be flat, not upturned. The candlestick was made in the 13th century, perhaps in Lorraine. Height 19 cm. *Victoria & Albert Museum.*

7 A 13th-century bronze pricket candlestick, possibly from Lorraine. It has a three-footed base and a knop at the lower end of the stem. The cast ornament is pierced and the drip-pan at the top is curiously decorated with three lugs. Height 15.2 cm. *Victoria & Albert Museum.*

8 The designer of this 13th-century German brass candlestick used his imagination in making it in the form of a mythical human-cum-animal. It is a variation on the classical centaurs, who dwelt in the mountains of Thessaly and appear in the writings of Homer. The flower-like candle-holder has lost its pricket. Height 14.6 cm. *Victoria & Albert Museum.*

9 A 13th-century Netherlands bronze
candlestick. The candle-holder pro-
trudes rather awkwardly from the man's
back. The group perhaps represents
Samson and the Lion. It is among the
numerous works of art bequeathed to the
Victoria & Albert Museum by George
Salting, an Australian-born connoisseur,
who died in 1910. Height 22.6 cm.
Victoria & Albert Museum.

10 A German brass candlestick in the form of an animal, perhaps a cross between a horse and an elephant, bearing on its back a building with a belfry and a castellated drip-pan. It dates from the 13th to 14th century. Height 17.1 cm. *Victoria & Albert Museum.*

11 Said to have been found in London, this small bronze candlestick dates from the 14th century. A very similar one is in the Guildhall Museum, London, and both are attributed to English makers. Possibly both examples came from the same workshop. A third variant, of comparable pattern but twice the size, is in a Dutch collection, its owner stating that it is of Netherlands origin. Height 8.1 cm. *Victoria & Albert Museum.*

12 The deep base of this bronze 15th-century candlestick is typical of others from Persia. Height 26.1 cm. *Victoria & Albert Museum.*

13 A late 15th-century Flemish brass candlestick with the stem and base attractively turned. The deep cup originally held a pricket. Height 42.5 cm. *Victoria & Albert Museum.*

14 Although at a glance they seem to be a matching pair, these 16th-century Netherlands brass candlesticks are not identical. They vary noticeably in the turning of the stems: extra rings have been introduced between the knops of the left-hand example. Heights 36.8 and 37.2 cm. *Victoria & Albert Museum.*

15 A brass candlestick found in London and possibly of local manufacture. It dates from the early 16th century. John Stow, in his *Survey of London*, first published in 1598, noted that the metal-founders were established in Lothbury, a street beside the present Bank of England. He commented on the method of finishing their wares 'smooth and bright with turning and scrating (as some do term it) making a loathsome noise to the by-passers that have not been used to the like, and therefore by them disdainfully called Lothberie'. This somewhat ingenious explanation of the name's origin is no longer accepted! Height 24.5 cm. *Victoria & Albert Museum.*

16 In the 16th century the prosperous Venetian Republic attracted many skilled craftsmen from the Near East who introduced ideas which gradually spread throughout Europe. From the Persian candlestick evolved the trumpet-shaped base and central drip-pan, as seen in this example. It was made in Venice during the 16th century, and the bronze bears an intricate all-over pattern of leaves, scrolls and strapwork. Height 17.1 cm. *Victoria & Albert Museum.*

17 This bronze candlestick could have been made in England or imported from the Netherlands, as the products of these countries were often alike. On the whole English examples were the simpler in design, but this one, like many others, could well have been made by an immigrant craftsman. Wherever it originated it was made in the early 16th century and was found in Northampton. Height 18.2 cm. *Victoria & Albert Museum.*

18 This brass candlestick was found in Guildhall, London. Of early 16th-century date, it could be English. Others resembling it are attributed to the Netherlands, but they are more elaborate in design, the stems with turned knops instead of being plain as in this instance. Height 16.8 cm. *Victoria & Albert Museum.*

19 A neat brass candlestick on a bell-shaped base which gives it great stability. Made in the Netherlands in the early 16th century. Height about 12 cm. *Victoria & Albert Museum.*

20 A 16th-century French Limoges candlestick made of beaten copper covered in enamel. The painting is signed with the initials I C, possibly for Jean Court, who died in about 1580. The circular panels round the base show the Labours of Hercules, and were copied from engravings made by a German artist, Heinrich Aldegrever. *Metropolitan Museum of Art: gift of Ann Payne Blumenthal, 1939.*

21 A pair of rock-crystal and silver-gilt candlesticks bearing the Paris date-mark for 1583-4. These were probably intended for use on an altar; the Louvre, Paris, has a somewhat similar, but un-marked, pair which were formerly in the Chapelle du Saint-Esprit, Paris. The custom of using candles in church is said to have derived from the period when the Romans were persecuting Christians: services then had to be held in secret, in hidden places such as the catacombs beneath Rome where arti-ficial light was essential. Height 54 cm. *Parke-Bernet Galleries, New York.*

22 A pair of late 16th-century Italian candlesticks, made of rock-crystal and silver-gilt like the preceding pair but different in size and shape. The crystal drip-pans in the present pair are engraved with flowering branches and sunbursts. Height 13.5 cm. *Mes Ader, Picard & Tajan, Paris.*

24 Wrotham, Kent, England, was once the site of a pottery at which this candlestick was made. Of red and white clay, it is dated 1651 and bears the initials of George Richardson, the maker. It is interesting to compare the candlestick with the late 19th-century pastiche in plate 117, which it would appear to have inspired. Height 24.7 cm. *Manchester City Art Gallery: Thomas Greg Collection.*

23 **A** satisfactory candlestick to describe, because it is clearly dated and its country of origin is beyond dispute. Made of pewter, it bears the date 1616 (seen on the front of the base in the illustration) as well as the name of William Grainger, who was steward of the London Pewterers' Company in 1620. Height 24.1 cm. *Victoria & Albert Museum.*

25 Brass candlestick with a wide central drip-pan and a hole (seen at the side of the candle-holder) for removing a stub of candle by inserting a piece of wood or metal. The top and base of the candlestick screw together, gripping the grease-pan between them. It dates from about 1650 and was probably made in the Netherlands. Height 26.6 cm. *Earl of Mount Edgcumbe.*

26 A mid-17th-century Netherlands brass candlestick with a low domed base and wide central drip-pan. Like the preceding example it has a hole in the candle-holder for removing a stub of candle. Height 20.3 cm. *Earl of Mount Edgcumbe.*

27 A 17th-century English pewter candlestick on a trumpet-shaped base with a central wide drip-pan beneath the short stem. Examples of this pattern also exist in brass and pottery (plate 28), all being made in the years about 1650. Height 29.8 cm. *Earl of Mount Edgcumbe.*

28 The 17th century saw a wide use of pottery coated with an opaque white glaze on which colours could be painted and fixed by firing in a kiln. The best-known and most prolific centre of production was at Delft, in Holland, but similar ware was made in England. This candlestick was made in about 1650, probably in London, and is painted in blue, yellow and green with a surprised-looking man seated among some rocks. Height 19 cm. *Manchester City Art Gallery: Thomas Greg Collection.*

29 A Dutch silversmith, Jan Arentsz van Rheenan, made this pair of silver-gilt candlesticks at The Hague in about 1655. Their history is traceable from the coat of arms engraved on the bases, and they were at one time owned by the grandfather of James Boswell, Dr Samuel Johnson's biographer. Height 16.5 cm. *Christie's.*

30 This pair of silver candlesticks with square bases and shaped square stems, resembling columns united by a central band, are ornamented with embossed designs of cupids, leafy scrolls and other motifs. They were made by Pierre Massé in Paris in 1675. Comparable examples were made in London by French protestant refugees who settled there after being driven from France by religious persecution. Height 17.5 cm. *Christie's.*

31 A pair of cast-brass candlesticks decorated with formal flowers, fruit and leaves enamelled in colours. The enamelling is of the champlevé type, in which the hollows to contain the colours are cast or cut below the surface. Such work was rarely executed in England, and surviving examples, dating from the late 17th century, are usually known as 'Surrey enamels'. Height 24.7 cm. *Sotheby's*.

32 A pewter candlestick with a wide domed base, the cluster-column stem rising to a flat drip-pan. There is a second drip-pan immediately above the base, but this is no more than a vestige of the earlier type seen in plates 26 and 27. It is of English make, about 1685. Height 24.7 cm. *Earl of Mount Edgcumbe.*

33 This late 17th-century English pewter candlestick shows the wide central drip-pan of the 1650s transformed into a bulge, or knop. The earlier trumpet-shaped base has become octagonal, almost flat and with a dished centre. Height 16.5 cm. *Victoria & Albert Museum.*

34 Like the preceding example, this candlestick is of English pewter of the late 17th century. Here, the central drip-pan has shrunk to no more than a slightly raised ring. Height 15 cm. *Victoria & Albert Museum.*

35 A pair of silver candlesticks on square bases with canted corners and turned stems. Cast and hand-finished, weighing a total of 23 oz Troy weight: a Troy ounce contains 20 dwt (penny-weight) and 12 oz make a pound. Made in 1703 by Pierre Harache, a silversmith of French origin who emigrated to London. Height about 18 cm.

36 Dutch influence endured in New York, formerly called New Amsterdam, for some decades after the English began to rule there. Cornelius Kierstede, one of the silversmiths working in the city, not only had a Dutch name but based his productions on prototypes from his native country. This is one of his candlesticks (of which the companion and a matching snuffers-stand survive) in the Netherlands style that was imitated also in England. Kierstede was born in 1674, died in 1757 and made the candlestick quite early in his career, about 1705. Height 29.2 cm. *Metropolitan Museum of Art: gift of Robert L. Cammann, 1957.*

37 The taperstick is a miniature candlestick made to hold a taper for melting the wax used in sealing letters, a method employed before the introduction of the gummed envelope in the 19th century. This group comprises tapersticks which all date from the reign of Queen Anne, and were made by a number of different makers between 1708 and 1713. Average height 11 cm. *Sotheby's.*

38 During the 18th century the Chinese makers of porcelain eagerly supplied European requirements. They carefully copied whatever was sent out to them, and this candlestick is a version of a Western brass or silver original of about 1720, painted in blue with typical Chinese patterns. Height 13.3 cm. *Victoria & Albert Museum.*

39 A set of four English silver candlesticks with shaped bases and stems. The square projections at the top of the stems are similar to those found on glassware: the so-called 'Silesian stem', presumed to have been introduced from Germany when George I came to England from Hanover in 1714 (see plate 41). The four candlesticks were made in 1718 by Edmund Pearce. Height 16.3 cm. *Christie's.*

40 These candlesticks were made by James Mitchellsone, of Edinburgh, in 1720. The work of the 18th-century Scottish silversmiths compares favourably with that executed in London. Although they were separated by a distance of several hundred miles, each followed current fashions while rendering them in an individual manner. The northern craftsmen often favoured an attractive simplicity of design. Height 17.1 cm. *Phillips.*

41 An English glass candlestick made shortly before 1750. Another example of the so-called 'Silesian stem' which became fashionable in about 1714 and remained popular until 1760 or so. Height 26.8 cm. *Christie's*.

42 This porcelain candlestick is another example of Chinese skill in copying a European model (see plate 38). The pink of the *famille rose* palette predominates among the painted colours, and some of the details are gilt. Height 16.8 cm.

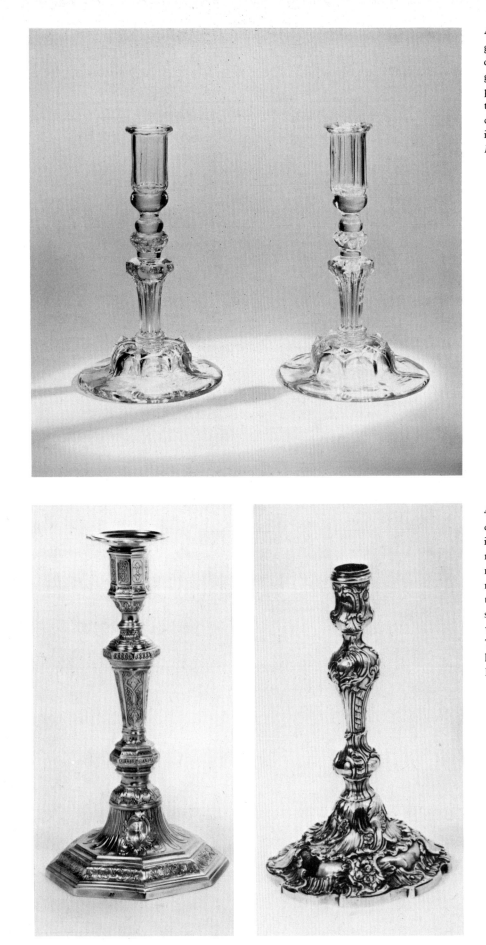

43 These mid-18th-century English glass candlesticks have domed bases, as do all standing articles, from wine-glasses onwards, until about 1800. The purpose was to lift clear of the surface the 'pontil mark', the rough scar produced during manufacture. After 1800 it was ground flat. Height 20.3 cm. *Delomosne & Son, Ltd.*

44 All the component parts of this candlestick are of hexagonal shape, and it shows the restrained use of decorative motifs. It is in complete contrast to the restless assymmetry of the succeeding rococo style, which was making a tentative appearance when the candlestick was produced, in 1737. The maker was Jacques Duguay, a Paris silversmith. The detachable nozzle in the candle-holder has been added at a later date. Height 22.8 cm. *Christie's.*

45 A silver candlestick decorated with scrolls, leaves and other ornament in the rococo style. It was made by Eliza Godfrey, one of the many widows who carried on the businesses of their late husbands. Mrs Godfrey entered her mark, the initials E G, at Goldsmiths' Hall, London, in 1741 and made these candlesticks in the year following. Height 24.1 cm. *Sotheby's.*

46 This set of four silver candlesticks was made in 1744, although their design was inspired by French examples of some 20 years earlier. They bear the stamp of Paul de Lamerie, the greatest English silversmith of his day. He died in 1751. Height 20.3 cm. *Sotheby's*.

47 These French rococo-style candlesticks can be dated with reasonable accuracy because they are stamped with a crowned 'C', a duty mark in use only between 5 March 1745 and 4 February 1749. They are made of bronze, gilt for the candlesticks and silvered for the figures. Their design is attributed to Juste-Aurèle Meissonnier, perhaps the man most responsible for introducing the rococo style. Height 26.6 cm. *Wallace Collection*.

48 The work of North American silversmiths is often distinctive in appearance, though embodying in its design obvious influences from one or more European countries. This pair of candlesticks owes much to France. They cannot be dated with accuracy, for, unlike in England and elsewhere, the new country did not have a marking system to indicate the year of assay and guarantee the quality of the metal. Makers, however, put their names to their products, and here the stamp is that of Jacob Hurd, 1702–58, who had a workshop in Boston. Height 15.8 cm. *Metropolitan Museum of Art: bequest of A. T. Clearwater, 1933.*

49 This pair of small candlesticks demonstrates the inventiveness of the mid-18th-century French metal-workers. The craftsman responsible has combined a pair of Meissen (Dresden) porcelain figures of canaries, and with the aid of ormolu has allied them with fragments of Japanese porcelain. Height 16.5 cm. *Sotheby's.*

50 A pair of English silver candlesticks, made by John Quantock in 1750, on shaped bases modelled at the corners with shells, the stems matching in design and rising to plain candle-holders with removable drip-pans. These last became a common and popular feature from the mid-18th century. Height 24.2 cm. *Phillips.*

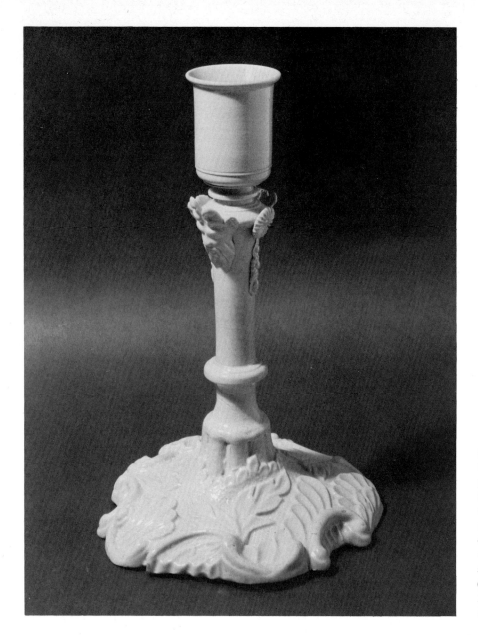

51 Salt-glazed stoneware, a very hard type of pottery, was the nearest thing to porcelain to be achieved by most Staffordshire makers. This candlestick is an example of the ware, dating from the mid-18th century. Josiah Wedgwood experimented with stoneware to produce his black 'basaltes', his red 'rosso antico', jasperware and other varieties (see plates 78 and 79). Height 21.5 cm. *Manchester City Art Gallery: Thomas Greg Collection.*

52 A set of four silver candlesticks of similar pattern to those in plate 50, showing how closely a currently popular design was followed by more than one maker. They bear the date-letter for 1753, and were made by John Priest. Height about 24 cm. *King & Chasemore, Pulborough, Sussex.*

53 These candlesticks were made at the French royal porcelain manufactory at Sèvres, just outside Paris, in the third quarter of the 18th century. They take the form of ormolu-mounted twisted columns, decorated with acorns and oak leaves in gold and green on a rich blue ground. Height 15 cm. *Victoria & Albert Museum (Jones Bequest).*

54 A mid-18th-century English brass candlestick with a decorated circular base and fluted column stem supporting a turned candle-holder. The engraved design incorporates leaves and scrolls. Height 32.4 cm. *Earl of Mount Edgcumbe.*

55 At one time all the surviving 18th-century English opaque white glass was thought to have come from Bristol, but now it is also known to have been made elsewhere. This candlestick, painted in colours with sprays of flowers and dating from about 1760, is attributed to a glass-works in South Staffordshire. Height 22.9 cm. *Sotheby's.*

56 A set of three candlesticks made of enamelled copper. The decoration comprises coloured flowers on a white ground, relieved by shaped panels of green with superimposed gilding. They were made in about 1765 at one of the factories operating in the Bilston-Wolverhampton area of Staffordshire. Height 28 cm. *Sotheby's.*

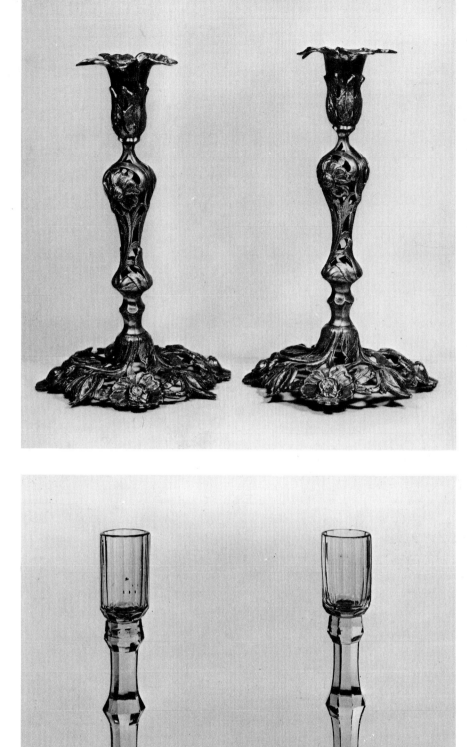

57 A pair of mid-18th-century Dutch silver-gilt candlesticks, cast in a pierced pattern of tulips, roses, leaves and scrolls. They were made in Amsterdam, and exemplify the international acceptance of the rococo style. Height 22.2 cm. *Phillips*.

58 A pair of English glass candlesticks, cut on all surfaces, from candle-holders downwards. The domed bases have notched edges, while the knopped stems are faceted. They date from about 1765. Height 23.5 cm. *Delomosne & Son, Ltd.*

59 A Sheffield plate candlestick in the form of a corinthian column, the stem and base ornamented with bands of husk and leaf patterns. Made by Thomas Law & Co, of Norfolk Street, Sheffield, in about 1770. Height 31.7 cm. *Sheffield City Museum*.

60 The maker of this pair of silver candlesticks was Ebenezer Coker, who made many other pairs of the same pattern. They date from the early 1760s, and their sober design, when compared to much other rococo then current, may explain their popularity. Height 26 cm. *King & Chasemore, Pulborough, Sussex.*

61 The classic corinthian column is
here rendered in enamelled copper. The
candlesticks are painted with scattered
flowers and, on the bases, with exotic
birds in landscapes. They were made in
South Staffordshire in about 1765.
Height 35.5 cm. *Delomosne & Son,
Ltd.*

62 A pair of English candlesticks in the form of corinthian columns raised on square moulded bases with bands of gadrooning. Made of paktong, an alloy of copper, zinc and nickel, brought to England from China during the 18th century, they date from about 1765 when the corinthian column was especially favoured (see plates 59 and 61). Height 29.2 cm. *Earl of Mount Edgcumbe.*

63 A silver candlestick in the form of a corinthian column raised on a stepped base with gadroon mouldings; made in Edinburgh, Scotland, 1768, by David Marshall. Height 30.5 cm. *Sotheby's.*

64 Like many other 18th-century English porcelain figures, the two on these candlesticks are of foreign inspiration. In this instance they owe much to Meissen for their form, and to Sèvres for the elaboration of their decoration. The man is holding a set of bagpipes and the lady plays a lute. They were made at the Derby factory in 1765-70. Height 22.8 cm. *Saltram, Devon: The National Trust.*

65 To contrast with the glistening cut-glass of the late 18th century, English makers also marketed coloured or white glass, porcelain and pottery. The gilt-metal mounted bases of this pair of candlesticks, dating from about 1770, are of shaped and decorated opaque white glass, a material sometimes mistaken for porcelain. Height 24.7 cm. *Delomosne & Son, Ltd.*

F

66 The Derby porcelain factory, which bought up the failed Chelsea concern, made these candlesticks. They are modelled with pairs of appealing white rabbits, backed by massed flowers and raised on bases imitating ormolu. They date from 1765-70. Height 24.1 cm. *Christie's.*

67 Some of the most popular themes for artists during most of the 18th century came from Aesop's Fables, shown in many forms – in books, prints and, in the present instance, modelled in porcelain. The pair of candlesticks was made at the Chelsea factory, then on the outskirts of London, in about 1765. Height 26 cm. *Victoria & Albert Museum.*

68 It is as unusual to find a complete set of eight old English silver candlesticks as it is to find them of a small size. This set are only 11.5 cm high and they are not tapersticks (see plate 37), as they are made to take normal-sized candles. From the workshop of Jonathan Alleine and date-marked 1772. Height 11.5 cm. *Christie's.*

69 A pair of French gilt-bronze candlesticks dating from about 1780. Each takes the form of three young boys supporting an upright cannon, in the mouth of which rests a cannon-ball. The latter is removed when the candlestick is in use. The design is attributed to the sculptor, Jean-Antoine Houdon, who was especially noted for his likenesses of children. Height 30.5 cm. *Wallace Collection.*

70 A silver candlestick of neo-classical pattern, ornamented with rams' heads, laurel festoons and other typical motifs. It bears the marks of G. Ashforth & Co, Sheffield, 1774, the year after assay offices had been opened in that city and Birmingham. Prior to 1773 hall-marking had involved sending goods to London or Chester, with consequent delay, expense and risk of damage. Height 29.2 cm. *Victoria & Albert Museum.*

71 A French gilt-bronze candlestick, one of a pair. The upper part of the base bears panels of trellis-pattern enclosing *fleurs-de-lis* divided by three dolphins, their tails supporting the stem and candle-holder. The presence of the *fleurs-de-lis* suggests royal ownership, and the dolphins allude to the Dauphin, the heir to the throne, born 22 October 1781. It is known that the candlesticks were supplied to Queen Marie-Antoinette for use at Versailles in that very year. Height 25.4 cm. *Wallace Collection.*

72 A Sheffield plate candlestick stamped with a classical pattern designed by John Flaxman. When newly-made and bearing a high polish, pieces like this closely resembled solid silver, though they differed not only in composition but in having no hall-mark. The Sheffield makers, however, often used their own marks which were deceptively like those employed at the assay-offices. Height 29.2 cm. *Sheffield City Museum.*

73 A silver-gilt candlestick in the French Louis XVI style, but made in Italy about 1780. It bears the mark of the city of Turin, at one time the capital of Italy. Under the base is engraved the arms of the royal House of Savoy. Height 27 cm. *Victoria & Albert Museum: Jones Bequest.*

74 Candlestick of silver-gilt, the stem with a central square section modelled with heads, and the candle-holder with a frieze of children playing. It is engraved with an inscription stating that it was made in 1783 in the royal jewellery workshops in Turin. Height 28.4 cm. *Victoria & Albert Museum: Jones Bequest.*

75   A pair of English silver candlesticks
of neo-classical design, the sparse ornament comprising florettes, leaves and
husks. The decoration is of the type
known as 'bright cut', which was carefully engraved at an angle so that it
glitters distinctively. The candlesticks,
which date from 1783, bear the mark
of the famed woman silversmith Hester
Bateman. She ran her late husband's
business from the year of his death,
1760, when she was herself 50 years of
age, and did not retire until thirty years
later. Height 29.8 cm. *Christie's.*

76 A pair of 18th-century Chinese (Ch'ien Lung period, 1736–95) jade pricket candlesticks of pale green colour. They are carved in the form of ducks with outstretched wings standing on tortoises in shallow bowls. The stone from which they are fashioned is extremely hard, and making such pieces took considerable skill and patience. Height 21.6 cm. *Spink & Son, Ltd.*

77 In 1778 Josiah Wedgwood wrote to his partner, Thomas Bentley, a letter which included the sentence: 'If one may confess a disagreeable truth upon this subject, it seems to me that *metal* is the only proper candlestick material.' Nonetheless he did make a number of candlesticks, of which this pair, dating from about 1784, is an example. In white and sage-green jasperware, the figures represent Summer and Winter. Height 25.4 cm. *Josiah Wedgwood & Sons, Ltd.*

78 The drum-shaped bases of this pair
of candlesticks are made of Josiah Wedgwood's jasperware, which he devised
and marketed in 1774-5. Wedgwood
foresaw the material as having innumerable decorative applications for such
purposes as the ornamentation of fire-
places and the backs of chairs, as well as
for scent-bottles and pieces of jewellery.
Height 31.7 cm. *Delomosne & Son, Ltd.*

79 A pair of pottery 'basaltes ware' vases and covers on shaped triangular bases. They are known as cassolettes, because the covers are reversible to reveal candle-holders, as in the example to the left of the illustration. They are each stamped WEDGWOOD. Height 27.9 cm. *Sotheby's*.

80 Two brass candlesticks of late 18th-century English neo-classic pattern, with tapering fluted stems and vase-shaped candle-holders. Although similar in design, the sizes are so different that it is most unlikely they were sold as a pair. Heights 25.4 and 27.3 cm. *Earl of Mount Edgcumbe*.

81   The town of Tula, in central Russia, was the site of the Imperial arms factory, the output of which included a small proportion of decorative articles. The candlestick illustrated was made there, of cut and polished steel: no fewer than twenty-seven separate pieces are held together by a central rod. The steel is inlaid, in the manner of woodwork, with gilt-bronze garlands of flowers on the base, stem and candle-holder. Height 31.7 cm. *Victoria & Albert Museum.*

82 This Leeds pottery candlestick, of about 1780, is in the full neo-classical style, in the form of a corinthian column with a decorative base. The latter is moulded with swags and rams' heads in relief; these and the capital of the column are glazed in green. Height 26.6 cm. *Manchester City Art Gallery: Thomas Greg Collection.*

83 One of Josiah Wedgwood's most successful productions was his cream-ware, or as he termed it 'Queen's ware'. Its great popularity invited imitations, and among the best of them was that made at Leeds, Yorkshire, England. This dolphin candlestick is a good example from there, made in about 1785. Height 30.7 cm. *Manchester City Art Gallery: Thomas Greg Collection.*

84 The Derby china factory provided the rectangular bases of this pair of candlesticks. They are mounted in gilt-metal and the stems are hung with pear-shaped drops. Dr Samuel Johnson visited Derby a decade or so before these candlesticks were made, and remarked that 'the porcelain made there is very pretty . . .; the finer pieces are so dear, that perhaps silver vessels of the same capacity may be sometimes bought at the same price'. Height 26.7 cm. *Delomosne & Son, Ltd.*

85 The qualities of English cut glass are eminently suited to lighting appliances, and these candlesticks prove the point. The swirl-cut vase-shaped stems, the cut candle-holders and the hanging drops all reflect and amplify the light. Height 29.2 cm. *Delomosne & Son, Ltd.*

86 A late 18th-century English brass candlestick with a part-plain stem and beaded base. The design is a variation on the usual classic column so popular at the time. Height 25.4 cm. *Earl of Mount Edgcumbe.*

87 A pair of Sheffield plate telescopic candlesticks. They were made with one or more sliding sections, and were the subject of patents from the end of the 18th century onwards. The pair illustrated is stamped with the word PATENT, but with nothing to indicate the inventor or maker. They date from about 1800. Height (closed) about 12 cm. *Sheffield City Museum.*

88 A pair of silver chamber candlesticks complete with extinguishers. They come from a set of twelve, of which each is numbered on a disc above the curled handle. Their maker was Matthew Boulton, of the Soho Works, Birmingham, 1803; a man remembered not only as a manufacturer of high-quality goods, but as the partner of James Watt, inventor of the modern steam-engine. Height 11.4 cm. *Sotheby's*.

89 A pair of silver candlesticks ornamented with ribbing and shell-and-leaf motifs, made by Matthew Boulton of Birmingham in 1813. They were manufactured from sheet silver and therefore are of light weight, so the bases are filled with a heavy substance (loaded) for stability. Height 33 cm. *Bearnes & Waycotts, Torquay*.

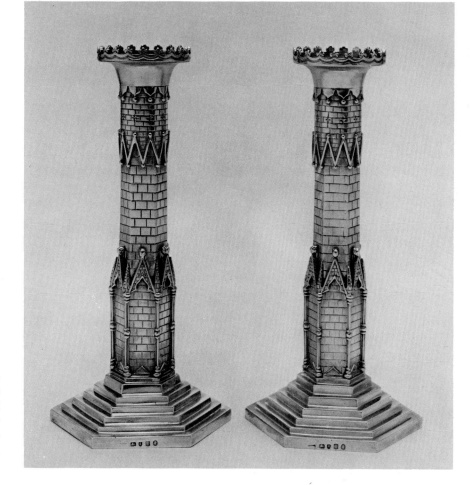

90 A pair of silver candlesticks in the form of Gothic stone towers. From time to time the Gothic style was revived, and these candlesticks date from 1814; they were made by William Elliott, whose workshop was in Clerkenwell, London. Height 28.6 cm. *Sotheby's.*

91 A Sheffield plate desk candlestick, of about 1815; the arm swivels round to adjust the position of the light and the base is weighted. *Sheffield City Museum.*

92 A Regency bronze chamber candle-stick, the handle resembling a French horn with a thumb-grip on the top, and the candle-holder patterned with formal flowers. This example retains its original bronzing, but it is not unusual to find that industrious housewives, or their servants, have painstakingly removed it with metal polish. Overall width 14 cm. *Earl of Mount Edgcumbe.*

93 A Regency brass chamber candle-stick, the tray with bands of beading and the curled handle terminating in a leaf. Brass and bronze articles, the former often gilded, were very fashionable at the time. Overall width 17.1 cm. *Earl of Mount Edgcumbe.*

94 Silver candlesticks of an attractive simple pattern; the fluted stems, plain pans and shaped bases conveying an impression of a classical column. They were made in about 1815 by Isaac Hutton, who worked in Albany, New York. Height 21.5 cm. *Metropolitan Museum of Art: bequest of A. T. Clearwater, 1933.*

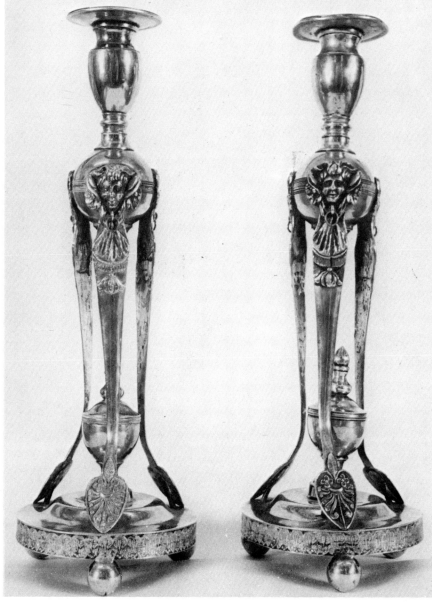

95 A pair of silver candlesticks in the early 19th-century French Empire style as rendered by a Spanish silversmith, F. Solis. Height 30.5 cm. *Bearnes & Waycotts, Torquay.*

96 A pair of bronze and ormolu candlesticks; the Oriental figures hold parasols hung with tiny bells. They stand on drum bases with square plinths ornamented with formal leaves and flowers, which are quite unconnected with the design of the figures: typical of the catholic taste of the Regency period. Height 31.1 cm. *Bearnes & Waycotts, Torquay.*

97 A set of four silver candlesticks in the form of two young and clean-shaven and two older bewhiskered Orientals, each holding aloft a bell-shaped candle-holder chased with flowers. The bases are elaborately patterned with shells, flowers, scrolls and other motifs, and they fall just within the true period of the Regency, 1819. They bear the maker's mark of Samuel Whitford. Height 19 cm. *Sotheby's.*

98 The Regency period in England was noted, among other things, for the lavish cutting of glassware. These candlesticks are good examples of the taste of the time and the technical skill of its craftsmen. They are richly cut with small diamonds and hung with round and pointed drops. Height 22.8 cm. *Delomosne & Son, Ltd.*

99 For use in places such as halls and passages, so-called 'hurricane shades' were made, and this early 19th-century English pair is among the rare survivors. The stands have diamond-cut bases, knopped stems and gilt-metal mounts, while the tall shades are delicately cut with continuous colonnades and rosettes. Height 56 cm. *Delomosne & Son, Ltd.*

100 The structure of these English glass candlesticks is barely visible, but the diamond-cut tall stems can just be discerned through their screen of drops. The bases are of gilt-metal and all the glass is cut in the elaborate style fashionable during the late Regency and in the reign of George IV. Height 39.4 cm. *Delomosne & Son, Ltd.*

101 These 'hurricane shades' are slightly later in date than the pair in plate 99.
The square plinths have stepped circular
stems with gilt-metal mounts, and the
shades are cut with a feathery pattern.
Height about 56 cm. *Delomosne & Son,
Ltd.*

102 An American glass candlestick of
about 1830 or so, the stem made by
blowing and the base moulded. The
moulding was executed by a pressing-
machine, the successful adaptation of an
earlier English invention. Bases of this
identical pattern were used for a number
of different articles. Height about 27
cm. *Delomosne & Son, Ltd.*

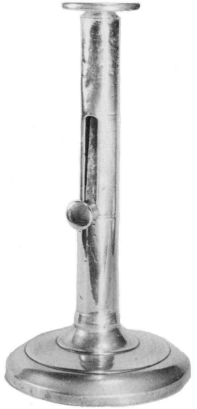

103 An early 19th-century English brass candlestick of simple pattern. The hollow stem conceals a sliding ejector operated by pushing upwards the button, so that the candle stub is removed without difficulty. Height 15.8 cm. *Earl of Mount Edgcumbe.*

104 Early Victorian English brass candlesticks, of which this is an example, were made in large numbers and in an infinite variety of patterns. The combinations of large and small knops in the stems varied with each manufacturer, and they differed from their 18th-century counterparts by their heavier appearance. This one dates from about 1840. Height 22.2 cm. *Earl of Mount Edgcumbe.*

105   In the early 19th century the use of pewter decreased. For tablewares it had been eclipsed by the improved pottery of Wedgwood and his imitators, but it continued in use for such objects as candlesticks. The example illustrated dates from about 1830, the plainness of the design being relieved by borders of gadrooning. Height 21.3 cm. *Victoria & Albert Museum.*

106 (top right)   A pair of silver candlesticks on bases modelled with shell-like ornament from which rise asymmetrical stems with small flower-heads in relief. They were made by an esteemed silversmith of his day, Benjamin Smith, of London, in 1836. Height about 26 cm. *King & Chasemore, Pulborough, Sussex.*

107   American glass is often as difficult to date as to assign to a specific source. These pressed-glass dolphin candlesticks have opaque white stems and bases with blue candle-holders, all decorated with gilt details. They are attributed to the Boston & Sandwich Glassworks, of Sandwich, Massachusetts, and were probably made between 1840 and 1850. Heights 26 and 26.3 cm. *Metropolitan Museum of Art: bequest of Anna G. W. Green, 1957, in memory of Dr Charles W. Green.*

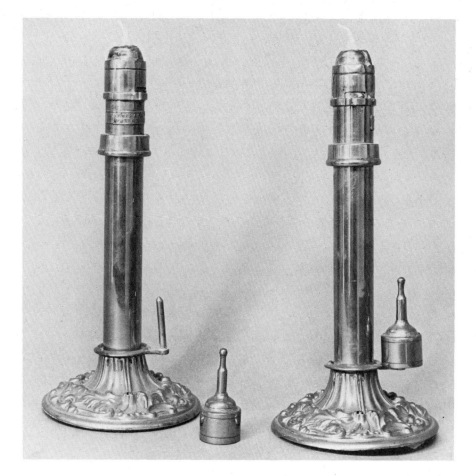

108 Pair of mid-19th-century English brass candlesticks and extinguishers, the interiors fitted with a spring to keep the light at a constant level. Each bears a plate embossed 'PALMER & CO PATENT' and they were presumably made by Palmer & Co, Sutton Street, Clerkenwell, who had a display at the Great Exhibition of 1851. The candlesticks are of about that date. Height 24.2 cm. *Private Collection.*

109 A pair of mid-19th-century pewter or Britannia metal chamber candlesticks made by Rosewell & Gleason, of Massachusetts. The firm was active between the years 1822 and 1871, and articles like these, of simple pattern, would have remained saleable during most of those years and are difficult to date accurately. Height 10.1 cm. *American Museum in Britain.*

111 A pair of pewter or 'Britannia metal' candlesticks made by Henry Hopper, of New York City, between 1842 and 1847. The two metals are similar in appearance, pewter being a mixture of tin with lead and copper while Britannia metal was made from tin and antimony. The latter often bears the maker's name, and in England the firm of James Dixon & Sons, of Sheffield, manufactured much of it during the 19th century. Height 25.4 cm. *American Museum in Britain.*

110 This simple black glass candlestick resembles some known to have been made at the Coventry Glass Works, in Connecticut, which was active between about 1813 and 1848. The design is ageless; similar forms were used in every country at one time or another. Height 12.7 cm. *American Museum in Britain.*

112 A bronze candlestick, the stem spring-loaded (see page 24), the square base weighted and the whole set in gimbals. For use at sea, where it could stand on its foot or have the latter affixed to a bulkhead, the candle remaining upright despite any motion. It is of English make, and like the examples on page 98 would have been in production over many years. Height 39.5 cm. *Private Collection*.

113 Glass factories active in the early and mid-19th-century copied each other's designs, in the U.S.A as elsewhere. The 'pillar-moulded' stem of this candlestick was a feature of examples known to have been made in the area of Pittsburgh, U.S.A., but it could have originated elsewhere. Height 24.1 cm. *American Museum in Britain.*

114 The town of Tunbridge Wells, Kent, about 40 miles from London, was a noted resort where people of fashion congregated for the sake of the health-giving waters. From the mid-17th century a woodworking industry had actively supplied visitors with distinctive souvenirs notable for their ingenious inlay work. This chamber candlestick dates from about 1860 and is characteristic of work produced in the town at about that time. Diameter 8.2 cm. *Mrs Una des Fontaines.*

115 A silver candlestick modelled as an aboriginal holding above his head an emu's egg on which is balanced the candle-holder. It was made by an Australian silversmith, Henry Steiner of 106 Rundle Street, Adelaide, and bears a stamp with his initials (H Sᵗ), a crown, a lion passant and an emu. Date-letters were not in use, so that the year of manufacture can only be guessed: Steiner was active between about 1858 and 1883. *Kurt Albrecht, Melbourne.*

116 The design of this candlestick was patented in the United States in 1870 and it was made by the New England Glass Company, of Sandwich, Massachusetts. It is of opaque white glass formed in a press-moulding machine. Height 24.4 cm. *Metropolitan Museum of Art: gift of Mrs Emily Winthrop Miles, 1946.*

117 This pottery candlestick proves that
not everything is as old as it looks or pretends
to be. Despite the date, 1640, clearly seen on
it, it was made in the late 19th century by
Edward Bingham, of Castle Hedingham,
Essex, an eccentric man who admired and
imitated the work of his predecessors. Height
21.6 cm. *Victoria & Albert Museum.*

Candles

Dr Johnson's definition of a candle was 'a light made of wax or tallow, surrounding a wick of flax or cotton', and those words written more than two centuries ago remain applicable. Although a number of changes have taken place from time to time, there is no basic difference between a candle made in the remote past and one of the present day.

Countries enjoying a high average temperature were unsuitable for candles, as the wax or fat forming them was liable to soften and bend in the heat. They were employed successfully throughout Northern Europe, but were usually unable to withstand the summers common to Italy, Spain and other lands bordering the Mediterranean as well as some farther east. For lighting that was required in such hot countries, the Italians and others relied mainly on wicks dipping in oil, which was held in bowl-like containers of various kinds.

Evidence that candles existed in the time of the Roman Empire occurs in the writings of the historian Pliny, who lived in the first century AD. He described two types: the one made of pitch with a wick of flax, and the other of molten wax into which a rush was dipped and the wax allowed to harden. Later, some Roman authors referred to candles of both wax and tallow. These two materials remained in use until the mid-eighteenth century, when the choice was increased and various improvements began to be made.

Tallow is animal fat, obtained locally, mainly from the carcases of sheep, or imported. In the eighteenth century supplies came principally from Russia, where oxen were specially fed to produce a notably hard fat, while in Victorian times Australia was a prolific source. In the home, surplus fat was saved in the kitchen, and one of the many tasks of a truly thrifty housewife was to spend time in the summer preparing for the long dark nights to follow.

The naturalist Gilbert White turned his attention to the matter in his *Natural History of Selborne*, published in 1789:

> The careful wife of an industrious Hampshire labourer obtains all her fat for nothing; for she saves the scummings of her bacon-pot for this use; and, if the grease abounds with salt, she causes the salt to precipitate to the bottom, by setting the scummings in a warm oven. Where hogs were not much in use, and especially by the sea-side, the coarser animal-oils will come very cheap. A pound of common grease may be procured for four pence. . . .

Additionally, White wrote:

> If men that keep bees will mix a little wax with the grease, it will give it a consistency, and render it more cleanly . . . mutton-suet would have the same effect.

The example of Hampshire folk was no doubt followed in many other places, the fat being used for making what were called 'rush dips'. Peeled rushes were dipped in fat, the pith forming a wick, the whole burning for an average of 30 minutes and according to Gilbert White's painstaking calculations costing precisely one-eleventh of a penny apiece. Five and a half hours of light could be obtained in this way at a cost of a single farthing.

The same writer concluded his description of rural parsimony with a short and sharp moral:

> Little farmers use rushes much in the short days . . . but the very poor, who are always the worst oeconomists, and therefore must continue very poor, buy an half-penny candle every evening, which, in their blowing open rooms, does not burn much more than two hours. Thus they have only two hours light for their money instead of eleven.

A mid-eighteenth-century authority stated that for making good tallow candles half the material should be sheep's fat and half bullock's. The ingredients were to be cut into small pieces, placed in a metal container over a fire and, when melted, a quantity of water added. This had the effect of precipitating impurities, and after the water was drained off the re-melted tallow was further cleansed by straining it through a horse-hair sieve.

The durability of tallow under adverse conditions was demonstrated by the scientist Michael Faraday when he delivered a lecture to children at the Royal Institution, London, in 1860. He showed his audience a candle that had been recovered in 1839 from the wreck of the *Royal George*. The vessel had sunk accidentally at Spithead in 1782 and the candle had remained submerged for a total of 57 years. Yet, as Faraday remarked, 'it shows you how well candles may be preserved; for though it is cracked about and broken a good deal, yet when lighted it goes on burning regularly, and the tallow resumes its natural condition as soon as it is fused'.

Conversely, above water, tallow often proved less long-lasting and then not only on account of its tendency to turn rancid. It was reported that supplies in lighthouses mysteriously disappeared, and when challenged the keepers said that they had been forced to eat the candles because of a shortage of more edible food. In contradiction to this it was alleged that the men had bartered their lights for 'strong liquors, their alternative excuse for shortages being that the candles had gone bad and they had had to throw them into the sea.

In the 1760s two kinds of tallow candle were available: dipped and moulded, 'the former are the common candles; the latter are the invention of Sieur le Brege at Paris'. Tallow, even when modified by mixing it with other fats or waxes, had a fairly low melting point, and candles made from it tended to bend and lose their shape in a heated atmosphere. The alternatives were made from beeswax, which not only retained their form under such circumstances, but burned more brightly and evenly while giving off a pleasant perfume. This last could not be said of tallow, although it had the undeniable attraction of being much cheaper.

Beeswax was obtained by melting honeycombs and straining the wax through cloths, 'which separates the dross and foulness, and lets the clear wax through'. The best variety was said to be of a yellow colour and with a fragrant smell, while it should break quite easily and not stick to the teeth when a little was chewed.

For candle-making beeswax was usually whitened by bleaching. To accomplish this, it was melted in hot water, pressed through finely woven cloth and then moulded into flat cakes. These were laid out in the open air and turned occasionally; so that sun and air did their work in rendering the material a semi-transparent white, 'and of an agreeable smell, like that of the yellow wax, but much weaker'.

In some countries vegetable fats or waxes were used in place of those obtained from animals and bees. The kernels within the fruit of the Tallow-tree (*Stillingia sebifera*) were employed in China. One of the numerous French missionaries who were there in the late seventeenth century was impressed by their use, and wrote of what he had seen. Of the tree and its fruit he recorded:

> But the wonder is, that this Kernel has all the qualities of Tallow; its Odour, Colour and Consistency; and they also make Candles of it, mixing only a little Oyl when they melt it to make the Stuff more pliant. If they knew how to purifie it as we do our Tallow here [in Paris], I doubt not but their Candles might be as good as ours, but they make them very awkwardly; so that their Smell is much stronger, their Smoak thicker, and their Light dimmer than ours.

He blamed much of the indifferent quality of the Chinese candle on the fact that they used for a wick a splinter of wood round which was wrapped a length of rush-pith.

The North American colonists took advantage of the native bayberry bush (*Myrica cerifera*), a variety of myrtle, which they found growing in New England. The berries of the shrub were gathered in the autumn, and the wax released by boiling them in pans of water. Bayberry was less highly esteemed than beeswax, but was considered to be superior to tallow. It was sometimes mixed with the latter to form candles of a stiffer nature than could be made with the tallow alone.

Shortly before the middle of the eighteenth century it was found that the cachalot or sperm whale was the source of a wax that was most suitable for candle-making. When the whale is alive a wax dissolved in oil occurs in the head cavities and in the blubber, but this separates after death and it can then be purified. Its qualities were described in an advertiser's announcement printed in the Boston, Massachusetts, *News-letter* of 30 March 1748:

> Sperma Ceti Candles, exceeding all others for Beauty, Sweetness of Scent when extinguished; Duration, being more than double Tallow Candles of equal size; Dimensions of Flame, nearly four Times more, emitting a soft easy expanding Light, bringing the Object close to the Sight, rather than causing the Eye to trace after them, as all Tallow-Candles do, from a constant Dimness which they produce. —— One of these Candles served the Use and Purpose of three Tallow Ones, and upon the whole are much pleasanter and cheaper.

At about the same date spermacetti wax was being used in England, where it was often mixed with tallow to produce a whiter candle. The spermacetti candle subsequently received an official blessing, when it was designated as the basis for determining candle-power: a unit in photometry – light-measurement. The (London) Metropolis Gas Act of 1860 stated that one c.p. should be the amount of light given out by a single spermacetti candle, of which six weighed 1 lb, burning at the rate of 120 grains an hour.

The next addition to the widening range of combustibles took place after a Frenchman, Michel-Eugène Chevreul, a professor of chemistry, carried out researches into the composition of animal fats and published a paper on the subject. This was in 1823, and as a result a new substance named 'stearine' was developed from the treatment of fats. From it was produced a candle that was comparatively inexpensive and proved a great improvement on tallow.

Later, in the mid-1850s, the discovery of huge supplies of petroleum in North America made it practicable to produce paraffin wax in quantity. The

Candle-snuffers in use. An engraving by
Jan Swelinck published in Rotterdam in
1627. *Mansell Collection.*

wax had been known earlier in the century, and once processes had been
devised for purifying and manufacturing it on a large scale it was adopted by
makers of candles.

The wicks of candles varied according to the wax used with them. For
tallow it was noted in 1764:

> The wicks are made of spun cotton, which the tallow-chandlers buy in
> skains, and which they wind up into bottoms or clues; whence they are cut
> with an instrument contrived on purpose, into pieces of the length of the
> candle required.

While, it was added, 'wax candles are made of cotton or flaxen wick, slightly
twisted . . .'

The diameter of the wick varied according to the amount and type of wax
or fat of which the candle was made. Tallow, for instance, required a more
substantial wick than spermacetti. The maker's judgement was exercised in
ensuring that the most efficient result was obtained; he had to achieve exactly
the right proportion of wick to tallow or wax.

Wicks were a constant source of trouble. In the course of burning they were
not completely consumed, and the accumulation of charred matter caused
molten tallow to run down the side of the candle: a commonplace occurrence
known as 'guttering'. At the same time the flame emitted black smoke, and
in extreme instances a high percentage of the tallow ran to waste. To avoid
this, it was necessary to trim the wick by cutting it to a suitable length,
removing the curled end which was the cause of the trouble. For the purpose
a pair of snuffers was employed: a scissor-like device with flat vertical cheeks
to hold the fragments of wick.

A late 17th-century English silver pair of snuffers in their original stand incorporating a candlestick. *Sotheby's.*

In the late eighteenth century ingenious steel snuffers were made with spring-operated blades and a central box to contain the charred ends. An unsnuffed candle not only proved wasteful of its own substance, but it gave only a fraction of the light to be gained from one that was properly cared for. Snuffing was reckoned to be needed at half-hourly intervals during burning, but only in the case of tallow candles. Those of beeswax, provided they were placed away from a draught, burned with minimal attention, and this gave them a marked superiority over the others.

Faults in the manufacture of wicks could also arise, and cures for them were sometimes given in books of household hints. One of them, printed in 1810,

reads:

> To remove a Thief in a Candle.
>
> It is well known, that a small knot of cotton, or as it is more commonly called, a thief, will occasion such an increased flux of the tallow, as to produce a deep guttering in a burning candle; and it is not less certain that a slip of paper, or any other substance of oblong form, about four or five inches by one, placed horizontally on the top of the candlestick, in an opposite direction, will almost instantly arrest the progress of the said thief, and prevent any subsequent effusion of the tallow.

With the introduction of stearine for candle-making it was possible to effect improvements in the manufacture of wicks and end the drudgery of snuffing. Instead of simply twisting the strands of cotton, as was formerly done, it was found that plaiting them gave the desired result. The burned portion was found to curl over and was completely consumed before it could do any harm. It worked perfectly in the case of stearine and paraffin wax, but not with tallow. The latter was soon supplanted by the newer substances with their snuffless wicks, and was finally driven from the scene.

Candles were manufactured by a variety of processes, which can be divided conveniently into four: moulding, dipping, pouring and drawing. All except those of beeswax could be moulded; the tenacity of the wax making it

First of four scenes at Price's candle manufactory, London, 1849. *Mansell Collection.*
The spreading and stripping department

impossible to remove the finished product satisfactorily from the mould. The latter was frequently made of pewter, but tin, iron and glass have also been employed. In New York, in 1784, Cornelius Bradford and Malcolm M'Euen, plumbers and pewterers, advertised that 'for tallow chandlers and spermacetti works, they make the best double polished candle moulds of all sizes'. While five years later, in the same city, George Coldwell announced that he had 'moved his Candlemould, etc., Manufactory from No 98 Gold Street in the swamp, to No 7 Beekman street, between Pearl and Cliff streets', adding that he had occupied the former premises for the previous 14 years.

The moulds were described clearly in an encyclopaedia published in 1855:

The moulds used in making mould candles are of pewter, and consist of two parts; namely, a hollow cylinder of the length of the candle open at both ends, and nicely polished on the inside; and a small metallic conical cap with a hole in the centre for the wick.

In some instances a number of individual moulds were held in a wooden frame, and in others they were made in a group secured at each end by metal plates. In use, the wicks were stretched tightly down the centre of each tube and held taut by wire or a stick. Then the molten tallow was poured in:

When the moulds are almost half filled the supply of tallow is cut off, the workman laying hold of the portion of each wick that projects from the point pulls it tight. This prevents the wick from curling and secures it in its proper position. The filling is then completed, and the frame [of moulds]

Steam boiling and engine house

put aside to cool. The candles ought to remain in the moulds until the next day, but it is known when they are properly set by a snapping noise produced by pressing the thumb against the bottom of the moulds.

The foregoing descriptions apply mainly to manufacture on a commercial scale, but many people, especially those living away from towns, made their own. While in 1754, again in the rapidly growing city of New York, John Ditcher, 'now living in the House of Mr. Jacobus Roosevelt's' offered his services in these words:

> He makes Candles and Soap for those who are pleas'd to find their own Tallow at reasonable Rates: said Ditcher has his Tools well fix'd after the London Manner. He would be glad of a Partner with a little Cash.

Whether the touching appeal in the final sentence produced an answer is apparently unrecorded.

Alternatively, tallow candles could be made by dipping, which was usually done in quantity by arranging the waxed wicks on a frame and lowering them into hot tallow. After each immersion the coating was allowed to harden, and the process continued until the candles were of the required thickness. Commercial dipping was performed with the aid of a balanced beam with an adjustable weight at one end and the frame of wicks held over the tallow at the other. The operator pulled down the beam at intervals, and knew he had done so often enough when the candles and the weight were evenly in balance.

Candle-moulding room

Beeswax candles had the wax poured over them in the following manner:

A set of wicks properly cut and twisted, and warmed at a stove, are attached to a ring of wood or metal, and suspended over a basin of melted wax, which is taken up by a large ladle and poured on the tops of the wicks, each wick being constantly twisted round its axis by the fingers; the wax in running down adheres to the wicks, and completely covers them. This process is repeated at intervals until a sufficient thickness is attained. The candles are then rolled while hot with a flat surface of box-wood upon a smooth table of walnut-wood kept constantly wet; this makes them truly cylindrical. This basting, twisting of the wicks and rolling is sometimes repeated two or three times before the candles are finished, but a skilful workman will cover the wicks with the proper quantity of wax without taking them down. If a wax candle be broken across, the annular layers, like the yearly rings in wood, can be easily counted, and their number indicates the number of times the wax has been poured over the wick.

Alternatively, the same writer stated:

The large candles used in Roman Catholic churches are made by placing a wick upon a slab of wax, bending this together and then rolling it.

The flexible tapers used in wax-jacks or 'pull ups' were made by a further method. The wick was unrolled from a drum and passed through a pan of molten wax, 'and thence through a drawing plate to a second drum'. The metal plate used was similar to that employed in wire-drawing, and the hole

in it corresponded to the diameter of the finished taper.

Tapers, as well as other forms of candle, were dyed in various colours. To the tallow or wax was added a quantity of red lead or vermilion for red, verdigris for green, gamboge for yellow, and lamp-black or ivory-black for black.

By the thirteenth century the French had established separate guilds for wax and tallow chandlers, and the same course was duly followed in London. The Worshipful Company of Wax Chandlers was incorporated in 1484, but as early as 1358 the Government had attempted to ensure that only un-adulterated wax was employed for the making of tapers and what were termed 'priketz': these last being intended for setting on metal spikes instead of in shallow cups. The arms of the Company show three red roses on a white chevron dividing three 'morters royal': the 'morters', or mortars, being squat pricket candlesticks presumably used in mortuaries.

In their earlier days the members of the Company would have been busy supplying their products for religious ceremonials of one kind and another. During the brief Papacy of Zosimus the Greek (March 417 – December 418) it was ordered that a wax candle should be blessed and lighted in all churches at Easter, and it was left there to burn continuously for the forty days to the Feast of the Ascension. For this purpose a candle of great size was necessary, and that used in Canterbury Cathedral in 1457 was said to have weighed 300 lbs. Another Paschal candle, lit at Norwich, 'was so lofty it had to be kindled by a light let down from the vault of the choir'. Further, it was ruled that the candles on the High Altar of a Catholic church must contain between

65 and 75 per cent of beeswax with the remainder of tallow. Other altars of lesser importance required candles with no more than 25 per cent of beeswax.

Further uses for candles in church services included the lighting of them for reading the Gospel, and the placing of a lighted taper in a child's hand at baptism. After the Reformation in England the use of candles in churches lessened as the ceremonials were simplified, and with the increase in general wealth under the Tudors the laity were able to afford artificial lighting in their homes. Because of this, the prosperity of the chandlers continued undiminished.

The Tallow Chandlers were probably of equal antiquity to their brethren of the Wax, and they were granted incorporation as a Company in 1462. As their name suggests, they regulated the trade in candles made from animal fats, although for a time during the reign of Elizabeth I they also gave their attention to soap, vinegar, bitter hops and oil. Members of the Company prospered not only from supplying households unable to afford the cost of wax or requiring something less expensive for everyday use, but from the sale of candles required for lighting the streets of the city. This duty, which dated from the fifteenth century or earlier, fell on each householder, who was required to hang a lighted lantern at his door as darkness fell. In the later seventeenth century street-lighting was assigned to contractors, and the individual occupier was liable only for the cost of the service.

Away from London the great houses, self-contained as regards most of their needs, would have provided their own candles. Beeswax and tallow were readily available and the task of candle-making would doubtless have been allotted to one or other of the numerous servants. Smaller homes might be visited by an itinerant chandler, who would have made a supply sufficient to last until the next call.

Such a carefree state of affairs did not endure, for in the eighth year of her reign Queen Anne introduced a tax on candles. It amounted to fourpence a pound on those of wax and a halfpenny a pound on tallow, payable on both imported and British-made goods. The tax was to remain in force for five years from 1 May 1740, and the stock-in-trade of dealers on that date, admittedly manufactured earlier, was also liable for the levy. The only exception made in the Act of Parliament was noted in the final section, which read as follows:

> Provided always, That this Act shall not extend, or be construed to extend, to Charge the Duties herein before mentioned, on such small Rush-Lights, as shall be made by any Persons, to be used in their own Houses only, so as none of them be Sold, or Delivered out, or be Made for Sale, and so as such Small Rush-Lights be only once Dipped in, or once Drawn through Grease or Kitchin-stuff, and not at all through any Tallow Melted or Refined. . . .

Successive Acts doubled the duties with effect from 25 March 1711 for 32 years, and from 1 May 1717 they were to continue in force forever. Simple rush-lights, as detailed above, remained free of tax.

Considerable evasion of the duties was found to be taking place, so an Act of 1712 tightened the regulations and subjected the chandlers to closer supervision than hitherto. They were now required to give prior notice to the Excise Officers every time they proposed making candles and at the same time state the quantity and size, while the actual place of manufacture had to be registered. Further, manufacture was permissible only during certain limited hours: from 7 am to 5 pm between 29 September and 25 March, and from 5 am to 7 pm between 25 March and 29 September. Abuses must nevertheless have continued despite these stringent rules, for additional regulations were enacted at later dates. Finally, in 1831 the duties were re-pealed, although in the year previous they had yielded a revenue of about £500,000.

Evasions of the duties were occasionally reported in the press, and the fines inflicted on convicted offenders must have deterred quite a few potential law-breakers. Two examples make it quite clear that the law was not to be broken lightly:

> 1751: 21 November. A tallow chandler was convicted on 3 informations: the first for making of candles, without notice, the penalty of which is £50, the 2d. for fraudulently and clandestinely removing the candles after made, without being charged, penalty £100, and 3dly. for making candles in an unentered place, penalty £200. he was ordered to petition for mitigation of the penalties.
> 1769: 9 May. A baronet was convicted by a bench of justices at Barnet, in the penalty of £3,100 for making his own candles; but the penalty was mitigated to £110 before the justices left the court.

More law-abiding, as no doubt were most other citizens, was Mrs Elizabeth Purefoy, of Shalstone. On March 1st 1737 she penned a short letter to a chandler in the nearby town of Buckingham. Her instructions to him were precise even if her spelling was erratic:

> Mr Sayer.
> I desire you would make mee so many pounds of candles as you have had pounds of fat of mee & make them the same size of the pattern wch will oblidge
>
> Your servant
E.P.

The retail cost of candles, including any duty payable, varied from time to time according to supply and demand. The year 1741 was noteworthy, for instance, for a shortage of tallow imported from Russia and elsewhere, and its price rose from the normal average of £45–£55 a ton to £60. Diaries and account-books sometimes record payments made for candles, although too often their writers merely note a sum of money expended without specifying the quantity of goods it purchased.

The agent of Sir Thomas Myddleton, Bt., of Chirk Castle, Denbighshire, made it quite clear what he paid for on his master's behalf when he entered for 6 June 1676:

> Payd Andrewe Hall, of wrexham, for a pound of wax candle,
> in yor Tyn box   0. 1. 6d.

On 29 January 1682 he made another admirable entry:

> Payd M^{ris} Rocke, for a wax candle, waigheinge 2^{li} & 2 ounces   6. 0d.

And again on 1 October 1686:

> Pd. Andrew Hill, of Wrexham, for 2^{li} & ½ of wax candle, sent
> to the Castle in July last   3. 4d.

John Hervey, of Ickworth, Suffolk, later first Earl of Bristol, was not always so explicit. On 5 October 1689 he noted:

> Paid for 2 pounds of wax candles, two wax books & five yards
> of yellow ribbon   10. 6d.

Again, on 19 November 1690 he was not very helpful beyond giving the name of the chandler from whom he made his purchase:

Paid Bend ye Italian for wax candles   2. 2. 0d.

He patronised the same man, this time probably spelling his name correctly, on 13 October 1696:

Paid Joseph Bindé ye Italian for wax candles and parmazan
cheese   7. 0. 0d.

Two of Hervey's later records are more informative:

2 February 1739. Paid Mr John Turner for 8 dozen of wax-
candles at 2s. 4d. per pound   10. 8. 0d.
8 February 1740. Paid Mr John Turner for 20 papers of wax
candles at 13s. each   13. 0. 0d.

Further evidence of costs is to be found in reports of London's Lord Mayor's Show of 9 November 1761. It was followed by the traditional banquet at the Guildhall, which was even more elaborate than usual because of the presence of the newly-crowned King, George III, and his bride, Queen Charlotte. The room in which the 1,200 guests were entertained was lighted by 'near 3000 wax tapers', and the cost of them was reliably stated to have totalled £92. 4s. The sum included a payment of £20 to 'Denny for lighting them'.

A few years later, John Parker, of Saltram, Devon, noted among his household expenses:

9 February 1771: Williamson, 20 doz. of candles   21. 0. 0d.

These would certainly have been of beeswax, and the date of their purchase coincides with that of the furnishing of the Adam-designed Saloon of the mansion.

An early nineteenth-century book of advice to travellers is informative about candles, noting both their cost and duration of burning. Coaching after dark would have been somewhat daunting in those days, and candlelight in conjunction with poor roads and the risk of meeting footpads would have done little to lessen its perils. However, the author gave some useful advice to those attempting it:

Lamps are generally lighted by Wax Candles, which weigh each a quarter of a Pound, and cost about 1s. each: if the Lamp is well made and well glazed, and no air gets in except where the air-holes are, they will burn about five hours: such Candles will burn about 7½ hours when still in a Room; but the motion of the Carriage, and the current of air in the Lamp, so greatly accelerates their consumption, that they will sometimes flare away in three or four hours.

There is apparently even less information about the one-time cost of common tallow candles, and it may be assumed that this was considered too insignificant to be worth recording. In Colonial America a few chandlers listed their prices, and in Boston in 1753 dipped candles could be bought for 4s 6d a dozen. Ten years later, in the same city, they cost 5s 6d. By the middle of the nineteenth century tallow candles were being sold in England for about 6d a pound, and snuffless stearine for 1s. There was then active competition from gas and oil as illuminants, and the candle had reached the peak of its popularity.

For use at certain types of work the candle was often considered to be superior to the oil-lamp. This was the case in the west of England, where the Cornish tin-miner employed a short length of candle affixed to his head-covering when he moved about, or stuck it to a nearby wall when he was working in one place. Likewise the boys who conveyed the broken ore along the galleries below ground had candles in the role of headlights on their barrows. Their use provided just sufficient illumination at the minimum cost. Nonetheless, it was recorded that the mines active in 1837 had used in the course of the year a total of 1,344,000 lbs of candles at a cost of £35,000.

Mention above of the lighting of London's Lord Mayor's Banquet at the Guildhall is a reminder that such occasions were sometimes the scene of what were in their day spectacular effects. Instantaneous illumination of a number of light-sources must have seemed almost a miracle in the days before electricity. It was achieved by connecting the candles together with a long thread of cotton which had been dipped in sulphur. When the cotton was ignited the flame ran quickly along it to give an impression of the candles bursting into flame simultaneously. This had been done earlier at the coronation of George II in 1727, when a guest wrote that 'the room was finely illuminated, and though there were 1,800 candles, besides what were on the tables, they were all lighted in less than three minutes'.

Nearly 70 years later, across the Atlantic in New York, a showman named Gardiner Baker, who advertised himself as the proprietor of the Tammany Museum, offered the public 'a very curious and extraordinary Philosophical Experiment'. It included the discharge at a distance of an apparently loaded cannon, and 'a candle will also be lighted only by turning a screw'.

During most of the centuries when the candle was the sole source of artificial light it was accorded the care it merited, and the precept 'Waste not, want not' conscientiously applied. The unburned stubs were carefully saved and in some homes a special container was kept for them. In the north of England this was known as a bark, having acquired its name, according to report, because simple boxes made from the bark of trees were first used for the purpose. In an account printed in 1774 it was stated that 'sometimes one sees it now at this day, but, in other houses, it still retains the name, though it be made of better material, of brass or tin'.

Candle-ends, whether saved in a bark or not, could be re-melted and used for making fresh supplies, or they might be burned to the very end with the aid of a save-all, a simple device noted as occurring in the mid-seventeenth century. Although there is no information about its precise form at that time, perhaps some type of metal pricket would have served the purpose. More recently, as late as the 1880s, the Staffordshire firm of Wedgwood listed a save-all made of their pottery. It was in the shape of a circular grease-pan above a plug that fitted into the candle-socket. On top of it was placed the candle, its base gripped by tiny metal prongs.

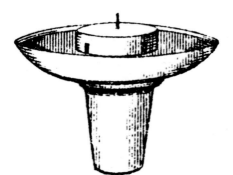

From the 1880 *Catalogue* of Josiah Wedgwood & Sons.

Bibliography

Kurt Albrecht, *19th Century Australian Gold & Silver Smiths*, 1969

Joseph Brasbridge, *The Fruits of Experience*, 1824

Joseph T. Butler, *Candleholders in America*, New York, 1967

A. J. Collins, *Inventory of the Jewels and Plate of Queen Elizabeth*, 1955

G. F. Dow, *The Arts and Crafts in New England, 1704-75*, Topsfield, Mass, 1927

G. Eland (ed), *Purefoy Letters*, 2 vols, 1931

Michael Faraday, *Lectures on the Chemical History of a Candle*, 1861

R. S. Gottesman (ed), *The Arts and Crafts in New York, 1726-76*, New York, 1938

—— *The Arts and Crafts in New York, 1777-99*, New York, 1954

S.H.A.H. (ed), *The Diary of John Hervey, First Earl of Bristol*, Wells, Somerset, 1894

H.-U. Haedeke, *Metalwork*, 1970

William Kitchiner, *The Traveller's Oracle*, 2 vols, 1827

L. le Compte, . . . *Journey through the Empire of China* . . ., 1697

(J. R. Liefchild), *Cornwall: Its Mines and Miners*, 1860

W. M. Middleton (ed), *Chirk Castle Accounts 1666-1753*, Manchester, 1931

William T. O'Dea, *The Social History of Lighting*, 1958

Charles Oman, *English Domestic Silver*, 7th edition, 1968

F. W. Robins, *The Story of the Lamp*, 1939

J. Tavernor-Perry, *Dinanderie*, 1910

A. J. G. Verster, *Brons in den Tijd*, Amsterdam, 1956

F. J. B. Watson, *Wallace Collection Catalogues: Furniture*, 1956

Josiah Wedgwood & Sons, *Illustrated Catalogue of Shapes (1880)*, reprinted 1971

Geoffrey Wills, *Collecting Copper and Brass*, 1962

—— *The Book of Copper and Brass*, 1968

Index